PEAR PEARFECTION

Sacramento River Delta Historical Society

Revised 2017

Compiled and Edited by Barbara Dahlberg,
Tom Herzog and Maryellen Burns

Cover Illustration Bob Miller

Sacramento River Delta Historical Society

Courtland Pear Fair Committee

Illustrations Bob Miller and from Jim Dahlberg Pear Label Collection Line

drawings are public domain or creative commons

Book and Cover Design

Maryellen Burns, Tom Herzog, and Gerry Ward

Cover Illustration Bob Miller

Published by Sacramento River Delta Historical Society

Table of Contents

ACKNOWLEDGEMENTS

Many decades ago, Barbara Dahlberg produced *Pear Pearfection*, a compilation of more than a hundred sweet and savoury pear recipes collected from generations of delta families, recipe pamphlets and regional pear associations. Long out of print, the Sacramento River Delta Historical Society (SRDHS) and Courtland Pear Fair Committee asked Barbara if we could revise the book for cooks eager to sink their teeth into nature's finest fruit.

Thankfully, she agreed. The book has been updated to assure easy to follow instructions and new recipes representing the early history of California's pear industry and today's trend toward eating local food, in season.

Our heartfelt appreciation goes to Barbara and all the contributors. We'd also like to acknowledge Barbara's husband of over 50 years, Jim Dahlberg, who generously allows *SRDHS* to produce a Pear label calendar from his massive collection, year after year. Jim and Barbara have worked tirelessly to support the Delta pear industry and the Pear Fair, a Delta tradition since 1972. Always held the last Sunday in July, the family-friendly festival celebrates the local harvest with bushels of pears from area farms, parades, pie-eating contests, and pear inspired treats, many represented in this cookbook.

Pear Pearfection would not be possible without the hands and eyes of many volunteers – Barbara Dahlberg, Maryellen Burns, Thomas Herzog, and Gerald Ward revised, edited, designed, and produced the book in record time. Our thanks also to the board of directors of the Sacramento River Delta Historical Society, the Courtland Pear Fair Committee, and California Pear Advisory Board who donated the funds to publish *Pear Pearfection* and to you the reader, who we hope find pleasure in reading, cooking and eating your way through these wonderful recipes.

July 2017

HOW TO SELECT A PEAR

- **Common Varieties:** Anjou, Bartlett, Bosc, Comice, Concorde, Forelle, French Butter, Reds, Seckel, Starkimson.

- **How they ripen:** Pears ripen best off the tree, so they are harvested mature but not ripe. After they go through a brief chilling period, the pears ripen from the inside out.

- **How to pick them:** If you are looking for a ripe pear to eat immediately, press a finger gently into the top of the pear just where the stem joins the fruit. If it just starts to give, the fruit is ripe. Don't buy pears that are soft, as that indicates that they are overripe and the flesh will be mushy and mealy. If you want to eat the pears in a few days, the top should still be hard.

- **How to store and ripen them:** Store pears either in the refrigerator or at room temperature. Depending on the variety, pears at room temperature will ripen in a few days. If you want to speed things up, place the pears in a paper bag with a ripe banana or apple — these other fruits give off ethylene gas, which the pears will soak up and then start to produce themselves, speeding up the ripening process.

- **Selecting a pear for cooking:** Bosc and Anjou varieties are tops at holding their shape and texture. Bartlett's are the most commonly used and available. Avoid Comice pears for cooking. Their tender, juicy flesh tends to fall apart when baked whole or used in pies. Smaller pears such as Seckel and Forelle are fine for cooking, but take longer to peel and core because of their size.

.

A BIT OF DELTA PEAR HISTORY

Eating a truly perfect, ripe, perfumed pear fresh from the tree, has been praised for thousands of years. Homer referred to them as "a gift from the gods." John Dryden opined, "When bounteous autumn rears her head, he joys to pull the ripened pear". And, while Ralph Waldo Emerson noted that there "is only ten minutes in the life of a pear when it's perfect to eat." Thomas Jefferson declared that the Seckel pear, grown outside Philadelphia, was the "finest pear I've tasted since I left France and equaled the best pear there."

Nowhere are those words truer than in the Sacramento Delta, an area celebrated for meandering, twisted waterways, historic river towns, a checkerboard of farmlands, and pockets of small family farms. With its ideal climate and soil, the Delta is one of the nation's primary supplier of pears, especially the Bartlett. Stretching south of Sacramento from Freeport to Rio Vista, it provides half the state's Bartlett harvest, which typically starts in early July. Local pear growers, many of whose families arrived with the gold rush, like to boast of their century-old groves and six generations preserving the Delta pears heritage.

The first pears came to California in 1701. Father Junípero Serra and other Franciscan fathers brought seedlings to the northern missions and created orchards in 1769 that fed a growing desire for fresh fruit. Pears made their way to Sacramento in late 1841, when John Sutter took control of Fort Ross's orchard, teeming with more than 260 fruit trees including 207 apple trees, 29 peach trees, 10 pear trees, 10 quince trees, and 8 cherry trees. His dreams of an agricultural paradise would be frustrated when John Bidwell traveled to San Rafael to secure additional seedlings of mission pear trees, and casually spread the word of the discovery of gold.

As news spread, thousands of prospective gold miners traveled by sea or over land in pursuit of wealth. After the initial invasion of 1849, many recognized that wealth could accrue more readily by turning to agriculture and other businesses to feed the burgeoning population. Eager young men brought new vegetable and fruit varieties from the east coast. Commercial production soon began on the lower slopes of the Sierra Nevada, along the California coast and in the Sacramento Valley.

The industry soon expanded. Nurseryman A.P. Smith created the first important nursery in California, planting Seckel and Bartlett pears in 1850. A.E. Warren and Sons Garden and Nursery of Sacramento became the first to issue a nursery catalog in California in 1853. Fifty-three varieties of pears are listed including Bartlett, Beurre Diel, Easter Beurre, Flemish Beauty, Forelle, Gout Morceau, Louise bonne d'Jersey, Seckel, Urbaniste and Winter Nelis. By 1856 he lists 76 pear varieties. That same year Charles W. Reed's Sacramento nursery brought trees and more seed. As the first large scale commercial fruit industry emerged, improved waterways led to the rapid increase in production. Paddlewheel steamboats plied the waterways delivering fruit from farmers, fruit packers and canneries between Sacramento and San Francisco. The completion of the transcontinental railroad allegedly allowed Reed to ship the first carload of pears to the east from California in 1869.

The Bartlett pear soon became the most popular and abundant grown in Courtland and other small towns between Sacramento and Isleton. They were the first ripe pears in the country, shipped soon after July 4th and available fresh throughout the summer. The sweetest, juiciest and most flavorful, they ripened at room temperature, could be canned, cooked, juiced, made into brandy or sliced for eating.

The Delta wasn't alone in pear growing. Other areas included the Clear Lake district of Lake County, Mendocino County, the Suisan Valley, Santa Clara, San Jose, and the Sierra foothills.

Growers discovered that getting the fruit to the marketplace was hard to hit right, difficult to pick at the point of perfection. They formed marketing alliances including the California Pear Growers Association. As the industry matured in the 1920s they promoted the industry worldwide. Improvements in science, grafting, and cannery practices led to success with the Bartlett, Bosc, Starkimson, Forelle, Comice, Taylors Gold, Seckel, Red Pear and the Asian Pear. '

Over the years some of the pear acreage in the Sacramento Delta transitioned to wine grapes and periods of drought and warmer winters impacted yield many years. Luckily, as this book is being finished, the California Pear Advisory Board estimates that 2017s California pear crop will increase 36% from last year. Most of California's 60 plus pear farms are family operations. With pride, a new generation of young people are coming home to the family farm to continue a long tradition. Another long-held tradition is the annual Courtland Pear Festival, held the last Sunday in July. The festival began in 1972 as a way for the citizens of the Delta to come together as a community. Organized and run by a committee of local volunteers, it has something for every taste with food booths featuring pear-centered pies, sausages, barbeque, breads, ice creams, cakes, pear martinis and mimosas and thousands of visitors from throughout the country.

NOTES ON THE ORIGINAL RECIPES

Every home cook has at least one of them tucked into a drawer, or a stack of them next to the bed – a community cookbook, splattered with batter, juice-stained, edges turned over to a favorite recipe. The kind of book you turn to when you need to bring a dish to the office potluck, are looking for a new sweet to share with friends, or want to read to get a taste of what foods were served way back when.

Pear Pearfection will provide all of that, and more. When Barbara Dahlberg decided to gather pear recipes from friends, neighbors and the Delta pear associations in the mid-seventies, her aim was to promote the Courtland Pear Fair and local Delta growers. The recipes she collected might have been handed down in the family for generations, an adaptation of a beloved friends dish, or a new recipe created to use local, seasonal ingredients at their best.

The original featured more than 200 pear recipes for every season and every occasion, representing the best home cooking in the area. Every recipe had been tested by a home cook and countless eaters at potlucks, holidays and birthdays. Barbara tested many of the recipes anyway, adapted them when she could, decreased the amount of lemon or sugar to make sure a recipe wasn't too sweet or too sour. She added cinnamon or ginger to spice things up, adjusted the amount of flour to get the texture right and otherwise tasted each dish to make the recipe her own and to her families' taste.

Of course, we don't suffer from the illusion that you are going to make every recipe, unless you are a fanatic, like Julie Powell who cooked all 524 recipes in Julia Child's *Mastering the Art of French Cooking*. Some of them are more than a hundred years old and might be difficult to reproduce. Others might seem too complicated or not as healthy as you like. However, there are a lot of instant classics scattered throughout, with a wonderful balance of flavors and textures and straight forward enough to adapt as a household standard. Play around with them. If a dish doesn't come out quite right, change it. Want to make it healthier? Consider using half the butter, shortening or oil. Most recipes taste just as good with reduced sugar or salt. Don't be afraid to change it and make it your own.

A NOTE ON THE 2017 ADDITIONS

Pear harvest season in the Sacramento Delta begins on the cusp of summer, just as asparagus season is waning, when strawberries, blackberries, peaches, and plums perfume the air and wine grapes dangle on lattices of trellised vines. Here, it may last for just a few weeks, but with pears harvested somewhere in the world all four seasons, adding fresh pears to salads or salsa, in a pie, or into ice cream can become a daily treat. Prefer to eat local? Delta canned pears are available all year round and make a great addition to pear cakes, breads, muffins, and hundreds of other dishes, limited only by your own imagination.

We've included a smattering of new recipes to this edition of **Pear Pearfection**. Some are historic, gathered from the region's earliest cookbooks, starting with **The Sacramento Ladies Kitchen Companion** in 1872 and ending with **Home Cookin': Delta Young Women's Club** in 1996.

Others were gathered at a series of events for *We Are Where We Eat*, a project to capture the stories of the people who grow, cook, and serve the food we eat. We received hundreds of heirloom recipes whose flavors describe another time and place and contemporary dishes that accommodate today's spur-of-the-moment cook and take advantage of widely available, fresh, local ingredients. We also heard stories of growing up in the city and going to the Delta to gather fresh pears at a road side stand, or accounts about working seasonally in the canneries and packing plants. One of our favorite stories was told by Kathryn Beltrami who remembers her father climbing a ladder and putting a bottle over a tiny pear, so that when it grew bigger he could retrieve it, pour alcohol in and make pear brandy, bottles of which she still has on hand.

We heard not only from the families of growers who have farmed pears for generations but generations of farm laborers who have worked the orchards and created their own twists on treasured recipes. A Mexican woman, who has lived and cooked on a pear farm for more than twenty years, makes salsa with chopped pears, red onion, serrano chili, and mint combined with olive oil and lime. A Japanese cannery worker, now in his eighties, remembered his grandmother making stewed Asian pears with honey and ginger when he got a sore throat. And, we heard from many others who loved everything connected with a pear, how it looks, how it tastes, and how delicious it is served with a shaving of Parmigiana Reggiano cheese or cooked in a delicious delta pear tamale.

Food journalist Amanda Hesser argues that by cooking, we make a statement of who we are and how we want to be remembered. That can be said about the contributors to **Pear Pearfection**, who submitted recipes that spoke to their own tastes and heritage. *Strawberry and Pear Cocktail, Italian Pear Chicken Salad, Spiced Pork Roast with Pears* showcase not only pears, canned and fresh, but a wide variety of fresh vegetables and fruits, poultry, pork, and local rice, grains, and dairy products, used in unique and varied ways.

All community cookbooks are informal histories of people and place told through their recipes, so though we didn't include the stories we gathered, each recipe tells a story nonetheless. We hope you agree that this cookbook paints a picture of what's cooking – and who's doing the cooking – in Delta kitchens and conveys a strong sense of place.

Nothing can replace the feel of turning the pages of a real book, especially a cookbook. So, we invite you to go to your local public market, farmer's market, local grocery store or roadside stand, and try these recipes out. Spatter it all you want, dog ear the pages, write notes in the margins, and pass this book on to all your friends. Or best yet, buy them their own copy.

APPETIZERS AND DRINKS

PEAR SNACK DIP

1 (16 ounce.) can pears
1 (3 ounce) package cream cheese
1 (5 ounce) jar sharp cheddar cheese spread
1/2 cup heavy cream
1 cup chopped cashews
1/2 cup finely chopped dates

Drain and chop pears, reserving 1/3 cup syrup. Blend syrup with cheeses. Whip cheeses with heavy cream until smooth. Stir in pears, dates and cashews. Serve chilled with crackers.

YOGURT DIP

Flavor yogurt with a little grated Parmesan cheese, grated orange rind, and savory. Chill. Core and slice pears, coat with orange juice and arrange on plates with a little watercress and fresh strawberries. Dip fruit into chilled dip.

STUFFED GOUDA DIP

1 small round (8 ounce) Gouda cheese
1/2 cup real mayonnaise
1/3 cup orange juice
1/4 teaspoon basil, crumbled
Few dashes white pepper
Paprika
Chicory
2 fresh ripe pears
Lemon juice

Slice rind off top of cheese. Scoop out cheese, removing all from wax rind if possible, keeping rind intact. Coarsely chop the scooped-out cheese and combine in blender with mayonnaise, orange juice, basil and pepper. Whirl until smooth. Spoon into rind and mound high. (Reserving any remaining mixture to add after guests have eaten some.) Sprinkle with paprika. Place in center of platter with chicory at base. Halve and core pears. Cut halves into lengthwise slices and coat with lemon juice. Arrange slices cut side down around cheese to be used as dippers. Makes 1 1/2 cups cheese filling.

STRAWBERRY AND PEAR COCKTAIL

1 basket strawberries
1 medium can (1 pound) pears, chilled
1/2 teaspoon finely grated orange peel
1 tablespoon lime juice
1/2 cup orange juice (1 orange)
Pinch of salt

Wash and hull berries; cut in quarters if large. Drain syrup from pears and save; cut pears into pieces about the same size of the strawberries. Combine berries and pears and spoon into 6 cocktail glasses. Combine the pear syrup, grated orange peel, lime juice, orange juice and salt and pour over fruit. Chill. Serves 6.

TOMATO-PEAR COCKTAIL

1 medium size fresh ripe pear
1 can (6 ounce) tomato juice
1/2 cup crushed ice
1 tablespoon lemon juice
1/16 teaspoon dill weed
1/16 teaspoon celery salt

Pare, core and dice pear to measure 1 1/2 cups. Turn into blender jar; add remaining ingredients. Blend smooth. Makes 4 4oz. servings, about 35 calories per serving.

PINK PEAR FROST

1 fresh pear
1/4 cup low-calorie Cranapple juice cocktail
1/4 cup plain low-fat yogurt

Peel, core and slice pear. In a blender jar combine all ingredients; blend until smooth. Makes one 8-ounce serving.

PEAR BRUNCH FIZZ

1 large fresh ripe pear
1 cup finely crushed ice
1/2 cup heavy cream
2 egg whites
1/4 cup gin (2 ounces)
2 tablespoons fresh lime juice
2 tablespoons superfine sugar

Pare, core and dice pear to measure 1 1/2 cups. Turn into blender with all the rest of the ingredients. Whirl until well blended. Makes 4 servings.

PEAR-BUTTERMILK PICK-UP

1 large fresh ripe pear
1 cup buttermilk
1 large egg
2 tablespoons undiluted orange juice concentrate Pare, core and dice pear. Turn into blender jar with the rest of the ingredients. Process until smooth. Makes 2 (10 ounce) servings, about 170 calories per serving.

PEAR YOGURT DRINK

1 large ripe pear
1 (8 ounce) container raspberry flavored yogurt
2 tablespoons wheat germ
2 large eggs
1/2 cup milk *
1 tablespoon lemon juice

Pare, core and dice pear. Turn into blender and blend until finely pureed. Add all remaining ingredients and blend smooth. Pour into glasses. (12 ounce) Makes 2 servings about 1 1/2 cups each.
* For a thinner drink, milk may be increased.

CARIBBEAN SHAKE

1 large fresh ripe pear
1/2 teaspoon instant coffee granules
3/4 cup milk
1 cup chocolate ice cream
2 tablespoons light rum
1 tablespoon sugar or honey

Pare, core and dice pear to measure 1 1/2 cups. Turn into blender. Dissolve coffee in milk. Add to blender along with all remaining ingredients and blend until smooth and creamy. Makes 2 (9 ounce) servings.

SALADS

S A L A D

FRUIT-NUT GELATIN BOWL

2 cups sliced fresh peaches or orange sections
1 No. 303 can pear halves, quartered
1 package orange-flavored gelatin (3 ounce)
1 cup boiling water
1/2 cup snipped pitted dates
1/2 cup chopped walnuts

1/2 cup heavy cream, whipped; or 1/2-pint ice cream Arrange peaches and drained pears (save juice) in bottom of 10 x 6 x 2 inch dish. Dissolve Jell-O in boiling water; add 1 cup juice. Pour 1 cup Jell-O over fruit. Refrigerate until set. Mix dates and nuts with rest of Jell-O; when partly set, spoon over fruit layer. Refrigerate until set. To serve, cut into squares with fruit side up, top with chipped cream of ice cream.

MOLDED FRUIT SALAD

1 (3-ounce) package lemon Jell-O
1 cup boiling water
2/3 cup fruit juice from pears
1 cup pineapple
2 bananas sliced
1/4 cup chopped maraschino cherries
3/4 cup diced canned pineapple
3/4 cup diced canned pears
1/4 cup chopped walnuts

Add boiling water to Jell-O. Stir until Jell-O is dissolved. Add fruit juice. Chill until slightly thickened. Add prepared fruit and nuts to jell and mix. Pour into Jell-O mold. Chill until set. Unmold on plate of salad greens. Serve with fruit salad dressing of your choice.

MOLDED CRANBERRY PEAR SALAD

2 envelopes unflavored gelatin
2 cups cranberry juice cocktail
1 can (16 ounce.) whole berry cranberry sauce
1 can (1 pound, 14 ounces.) pear halves, drained & diced
1/2 cup finely chopped celery
1 large apple, peeled, cored and shredded
1 cup bite size salad greens

Stir gelatin into 1 cup cranberry juice. Place mixture over low heat and stir until gelatin is dissolved. Stir into remaining cranberry juice. Add whole berry sauce and stir. Chill until thickened and consistency of unbeaten egg whites. Fold in pears, celery and shredded apple. Pour into 1 1/2 quart mold. Chill until firm. Unmold on a bed of bite size salad greens. Serve garnished with mayonnaise. Serves 8.

CARDINAL PEAR MOLD

1 package (3 ounce) Jell-O, cherry or black cherry
1 cup boiling water
1 can (1pound) pear halves
1/2 teaspoon grated orange rind (optional)
1/8 teaspoon ground ginger
2 tablespoons orange juice

Dissolve Jell-O in boiling water. Drain pears, measuring juice to make 3/4 cup, adding a little water if necessary. Add juice, orange rind, ginger and orange juice to Jell-O. Pour into mold. When partially set, add pear halves. Return to refrigerator and chill. Unmold on plate and serve. Serves 4 to 6.

GINGER-UPPER

1 package (3 ounce) raspberry or lemon Jell-O
1 cup boiling water
1 1/2 teaspoon lemon juice
1 cup ginger ale
1 cup diced fresh pears

Dissolve Jell-O in boiling water. Add lemon juice and ginger ale. Chill until very thick. Add diced pears. Spoon into Jell-O mold. Chill until very firm. Unmold on plate lined with fresh salad greens. Serves 6

PEAR AND AVOCADO MOLD

2 avocadoes, diced
1 can pears, drained and diced
2 packages (3 ounce) lime Jell-O
1 package (3 ounce) cream cheese

Prepare 1 package Jell-O and pour over diced pears and avocadoes. Chill until firm. Prepare second package of Jell-O. Add softened cream cheese and pour over fruited Jell-O. Serve with dressing.

Dressing

4 egg yolks
4 tablespoons vinegar
1 tablespoon sugar
1 teaspoon dry mustard
salt and paprika
12 large marshmallows
1 cup whipped cream or 1 cup whipped topping

Mix egg yolks, vinegar, sugar, mustard, salt and paprika together in a double boiler. Cook until thickened. Remove from heat and add 12 marshmallows. Cover pan until marshmallows are melted. Cool. Fold in 1 cup whipped cream. Pour over Jell-O and serve.

SHAPE-UP SALAD

2 cans (1 pound each) low-calorie purple plums
1 cup cold water
2 envelopes plain gelatin
1/2 teaspoon salt
1 1/2 cups low calorie ginger ale
2 tablespoons lemon juice
2 fresh Bartlett pears
1 cup seedless grapes
Iceberg lettuce

Drain plums, saving syrup. Halve and remove pits from plums.
Combine water, gelatin and salt in saucepan and heat, stirring until
gelatin is dissolved. Add plum syrup and cool. Stir in ginger ale and
lemon juice. Chill until mixture begins to thicken. Pare, halve and core
pears; cut crosswise into crescents. Fold pears, grapes and plums into
gelatin. Turn into 7-cup mold or 9-inch square pan. Chill till firm.
Invert mold onto platter (or cut into squares). Serve garnished with
fresh lettuce. Serves 8 or 9.

MINTY CRANBERRY PEAR SALAD

1 (1 pound) can jellied cranberry sauce
6 canned pear halves with juice
Green vegetable food coloring
Peppermint or mint extract
Softened cream cheese
Watercress

Several hours before serving or night before, place pear juice in deep
dish. Stir in few drops of green food coloring and 1 to 2 drops
peppermint extract. Add pear halves. Chill. Just before serving, cut can
of jellied cranberry sauce into 6 slices. Place slices in a circle on round
plate, edge of each overlapping the other. Drain pears. Place cut side
down to from ring inside of the cranberry slices. Garnish with cream
cheese squeezed through a pastry tube and watercress.

PEAR LIME SALAD

1 package (3 ounce) lime Jell-O
1 cup boiling water
1 cup pear juice
1 (3 ounce) package cream cheese
2 tablespoons mayonnaise
1 can drained, diced pears

1 cup heavy cream, whipped (may use whipped topping) Mix Jell-O and boiling water. Stir until Jell-O is dissolved. Add pear juice, chill until partially set. Beat until fluffy. Add softened cream cheese and mayonnaise. Fold in diced pears and whipped cream. Chill till set.

MINTY PEAR CHEESE SALAD

2 packages 3-oz. lime Jell-O
2 cups boiling water
1 can (1 lb.) pear halves
8 drops mint extract
2 packages (3 oz. each) cream cheese, softened

Dissolve Jell-O in boiling water. Drain pears, measuring juice and adding water to make 1 3/4 cups. Stir juice and mint extract into Jell-O. Set aside 1 cup Jell-O; pour remaining Jell-O into 1 1/2 quart mold. Chill until slightly thickened. Quarter pear halves and place in Jell-O, stir to blend. Chill until set, but not firm. Gradually blend the 1 cup reserved Jell-O into softened cream cheese; pour over Jell-O and pears. Chill until firm. Unmold on plate garnished with salad greens and sour cream. Makes 8 to 10 servings.

PEAR BLUE CHEESE SALAD

3 cups diced unpared pears
1 cup diced celery
1/2 cup broken walnuts
1 ounce crumbled blue cheese (1/4 cup)
1/4 cup sour cream
1/4 cup mayonnaise

Combine pears, celery, and walnuts. Blend blue cheese, sour cream, mayonnaise and a dash of salt. Toss lightly with pear mixture. Serves 6 to 8.

PEAR AND TUNA SALAD EXOTICA

2 cans (7 ounce can) tuna, drained
1 cup sliced celery
2 tablespoons pimiento strips
2 tablespoons diced candied ginger
2 tablespoons sliced pickled onion
1/4 cup slivered almonds
1/4 cup plain yogurt
1/4 cup mayonnaise
1/2 teaspoon seasoned salt
4 ripe pears
Salad greens

Carefully mix all ingredients except pears and greens. Core pears and cut into wedges with pear slicer or knife. Arrange wedges sunburst-fashion on greens-lined plate; spoon tuna mixture into center of each pear. Serves 4.

SALMON AND PEAR SALAD

4 small pears
3 tablespoons lemon juice
1 pound canned salmon
1/4 cup tomato juice
2 tablespoons chopped fresh parsley
2 tablespoons Worcestershire
Lettuce leaves
4 tablespoons mayonnaise
Pimento strips to garnish

Cut pears in quarters lengthwise, core. Brush with lemon juice. Place on lettuce-lined plates. Combine salmon, tomato juice, parsley and Worcestershire; mix well. Spoon mixture evenly on pears. Top each salad with mayonnaise and pimento strip. Makes 4 servings.

SHRIMP PEAR AND AVOCADO SALAD

1/2 cup white vinegar
1/4 cup salad oil
1 1/2 tablespoons Worcestershire Sauce
1 teaspoon sugar
1/2 teaspoon salt
1/2 teaspoon lemon pepper
3/4 teaspoon basil, crumbled
1/4 teaspoon pepper
1/2 teaspoon oregano, crumbled
3/4 pound fresh shrimp, shelled
Fresh Bartlett pear
1 avocado
Lemon juice
Iceberg lettuce

In saucepan, combine vinegar, oil, Worcestershire, sugar, salt and other seasonings. Bring to a boil, add shrimp and remove from heat. Cover and refrigerate for at least 4 hours. Halve, core and slice pear. Slice avocado into crescents. Coat pears and avocado with lemon juice. Shred lettuce and put into salad plates lined with large outer leaves. Arrange shrimp, pears and avocado over lettuce. Reheat the remaining marinade and serve with salads. Makes 4 servings.

PEAR SEAFOOD SALAD WITH CURRY DRESSING

1 can (6 1/2 ounce) crab or 1 cup fresh cooked crab
1 can (6 1/2 ounce) shrimp or 1 cup fresh cooked shrimp
3/4 cup real mayonnaise
1/2 cup dairy sour cream
2 tablespoons finely chopped onion
1 teaspoon curry powder
1/4 teaspoon salt
1/2 cup sliced water chestnuts
3 fresh pears
Lemon juice

Halve pears and scoop out cores with a tablespoon. Slice a bit off each half to prevent tipping. Sprinkle with lemon juice. Drain and combine shellfish and water chestnuts. Combine mayonnaise, sour cream, onion and curry powder to make dressing. Mix 1/4 cup of the dressing with the shellfish mixture. Mound onto pear halves. Serve on individual salad plates lined with fresh lettuce leaves. Pass remaining dressing. Makes 6 salads.

SALMON PEAR PLATE

1 can (7 ounce) salmon, drained
1 1/2 cups sliced fresh mushrooms
1 can (7 ounce) asparagus, drained
1/3 cup salad oil
2 1/2 tablespoons white vinegar
1/4 teaspoon salt
1/4 teaspoon dry mustard
Crisp lettuce leaves
1 or 2 fresh ripe pears
Sea Cream Dressing

Place salmon, mushrooms and asparagus separately in a shallow dish.
Mix together the salad oil, vinegar, salt and mustard; spoon over
salmon. Cover and chill for 1 hour. Line 4 salad plates with lettuce.
Pare, halve, core and slice pears. Arrange salmon, mushrooms,
asparagus and pear slices on lettuce. Serve with Sea Cream Dressing.
Makes 4 salads.

Sea Cream Dressing

1 cup dairy sour cream
1 tablespoon anchovy paste
2 tablespoons chopped fresh parsley
2 tablespoons capers (optional)

Combine all ingredients, stirring until smooth. Makes enough dressing
for 4 servings.

PEAR CRAB BOATS

3 or 4 fresh pears
Lemon juice
1 can (7 1/2 ounce) crab meat
1/2 cup mayonnaise
1 tablespoon chopped parsley
1 teaspoon vinegar
1 tablespoon catsup
Dash of Worcestershire
Dash of tabasco sauce
Iceberg lettuce
Lemon slices
Parsley

Halve and core pears. With melon baller, cut as many balls as you can from each pear half, leaving it hollow to form a boat. Take care not to break pear or cut through. Sprinkle with lemon juice. Mix together pear balls, drained crab meat, mayonnaise, parsley, vinegar, catsup, Worcestershire and Tabasco sauce. Spoon mixture into pear boats. Chill. Serve on lettuce-lined plates. Garnish with lemon slices and parsley.

CRUNCHY PEAR-CHICKEN SALAD

1 fresh, peeled, chopped Bartlett pear
2 1/2 cubed, cooked chicken
1/2 cup roasted, slivered almonds
1/4 cup diced green bell pepper
Pepper
Celery salt to taste

Combine and toss with 1/2 cup dressing. Mound onto 4 lettuce lined plates.

Dressing

1 cup plain yogurt
1/4 teaspoon. curry powder
2 tablespoons sugar
salt to taste

Garnish with lots of sliced, fresh pears and a few pimento strips. Pass remaining dressing.

ITALIAN PEAR-CHICKEN SALAD

4 fresh ripe Bartlett pears
3 cups cooked diced chicken
3 chopped green onions
2/3 cups diced celery
1/3 cup diced green pepper
1/2 cup sliced water chestnuts
3/4 cup mayonnaise
1 package (0.9 ounce) Italian salad dressing mix
1/2 teaspoon curry powder
Lettuce
Frosted grapes

Core and dice pears to make 1 1/2 cups. Cut the remaining pears into wedges and reserve. Toss diced pears, chicken, green onions, celery, green pepper and water chestnuts. Blend mayonnaise with salad dressing mix and curry powder. Add to pear and chicken, mixing lightly. Arrange reserved pear wedges on 6 lettuce lined plates. Top with pear and chicken salad and garnish with frosted grapes. Serve chilled.

To make frosted grapes:

Brush small bunches of seedless grapes with slightly beaten egg white. Sprinkle with granulated super fine sugar. Let dry on a rack.

ORIENTAL CHICKEN-PEAR SALAD

1 (16 ounce) can pears, drained and diced
1 (11 ounce) can mandarin oranges, drained
1 (8 ounce) can pineapple chunks, drained
1 (5 ounce) can water chestnuts, sliced
3 cups cubed cooked chicken
1 cup diced celery
3/4 cup mayonnaise
Salt and pepper to taste
1 teaspoon ground ginger
1/4 cup slivered almonds

Drain fruits and water chestnuts. Combine diced fruits, water chestnuts, chicken and celery. Chill. Blend mayonnaise, ginger, salt and pepper. Toss with chicken fruit mixture and top with slivered almonds. Makes a delicious luncheon salad.

TURKEY SALAD ROLLS

1/2 cup mayonnaise
1 teaspoon prepared mustard
1 teaspoon seasoned salt
1 teaspoon drained sweet pickle relish
1 tablespoon chopped parsley
16 small slices cooked turkey
2 large ripe pears

Combine mayonnaise, mustard, salt, pickle relish and parsley together. Spread evenly over turkey slices. Pare and core pears. Cut each pear into eighths. Roll one of the turkey slices around each pear slice. Skewer with toothpick and crown with small radish. Makes 4 servings as salad rolls.

PEAR SALAD NAPOLI

1 can (15 ounce) white or red kidney beans
1 can (15 ounce) garbanzo beans
8 cherry tomatoes
Small lettuce leaves
1 1/2 quarts torn lettuce
3 large fresh ripe pears
8 small sweet pickle chips
1 small sweet red onion, sliced
12 small slices salami
Napoli dressing, well chilled

Rinse and drain beans. Cut tomatoes in half. Line a large salad bowl with small lettuce leaves. Tear lettuce into bite size pieces. Halve and core pears. Slice one whole pear and toss with torn lettuce; add to salad bowl. Arrange drained beans, tomatoes, pickles and onion on top. Fold or roll salami and tuck into lettuce around one edge of salad. Arrange remaining pear halves around other edge of salad. Serve with Napoli dressing.

Napoli Dressing

3/4 cup salad oil
1 small clove garlic
1/3 cup garlic flavored wine vinegar
1 1/2 teaspoon dry mustard
1/4 cup honey
1/2 teaspoon basil, crumbled
3 tablespoons chili sauce
1/4 teaspoon oregano, crumbled
2 tablespoon. chopped green onion
1 tablespoon lemon juice
1/4 teaspoon dried dill

Measure all ingredients into blender jar. Cover and blend till well mixed. Cover and chill several hours before using. Makes about 1 1/2 cups dressing.

WINTER PEAR AND RICE SALAD VINAIGRETTE

2/3 cup rice
1 jar (6 ounce) marinated artichoke hearts
12 ounces small cooked shrimp
Lime Vinaigrette Dressing
2 winter pears, cored and diced
1/4 cup cubed Monterey Jack Cheese
3 tablespoons sliced green onion
2 tablespoons time juice
Radish slices for garnish
2 winter pears for garnish

Cook rice according to package directions until just tender. Drain artichoke hearts; reserve liquid. Cut artichoke hearts in half; reserve 10 halves for garnish. Cut remaining artichokes into bite-size pieces. Reserve 6 to 8 attractive whole shrimp for garnish. Combine hot rice, shrimp and 1/4 cup lime dressing, let stand until cool. Combine diced pears, artichokes, cheese, green onion and lime juice with rice mixture; toss gently. Place half of the mixture in deep 1 1/2 quart bowl, lightly oiled. Arrange reserved artichoke hearts alongside of bowl; fill with remaining mixture. Refrigerate several hours. Unmold onto serving platter. Garnish top with reserved shrimp and radish slices. Quarter and core pears. Brush with lime juice and arrange wedges and a few whole radishes around platter. Serves 6.

Lime Vinaigrette Dressing

Add salad oil to reserved artichoke liquid to equal 3 tablespoons. Stir in 1 tablespoon lime juice, 1 tablespoon vinegar and dash of crushed dill weed.

POLKA PEAR SALAD

1/2 pound bacon
2 tablespoons sugar
1/4 cup vinegar
1/2 teaspoon dill weed
1/2 teaspoon salt
1/4 teaspoon pepper
2 fresh ripe Bartlett pears
1 quart sliced cooked potatoes
1/2 cup sliced green onion and tops

Dice bacon, cook until crisp. Drain, saving 1/4 cup drippings. Combine bacon, reserved drippings, sugar, vinegar, dill weed, salt and pepper. Core pears; cut into chunks to measure about 2 cups. Toss pear, potato and onion with bacon dressing. Serve warm or cold. Makes 6 to 8 servings.

PEARS WITH GORGONZOLA

3 ripe pears
Soft Gorgonzola or blue cheese

Wash ripe, but firm pears. Halve and remove centers with a teaspoon. Remove woody stem part. Into each pear cavity, spoon about 2 teaspoons of softened Gorgonzola cheese. Cover and refrigerate, but bring back to room temperature about 15 minutes before serving. Makes 6 servings.

CHEVRE AND PEAR SALAD

4 ounces ripened chevre (goat cheese)
1 ripe pear
Lemon juice
Bibb lettuce, washed and dried
Dressing (below)

Marinate the cheese in dressing for 2 hours before serving. Line two salad plates with Bibb lettuce. Pare and core pear just before serving. Slice pear lengthwise in strips and rub with lemon juice to prevent discoloration. Fan out pear strips on lettuce. Remove cheese from dressing and cut into strips and arrange on plates. Spoon dressing over salads. Makes 2 main course lunch salads.

Dressing

3 tablespoons salad oil
2 tablespoons dry champagne
1 tablespoon wine vinegar
1 teaspoon Dijon mustard
1/2 teaspoon salt
1/8 teaspoon white pepper

Mix all ingredients together and refrigerate until serving time.

PEAR-CHEESE SALAD

Canned pear halves, drained
Greek Yogurt
Shredded sharp American cheese

Arrange pear halves on lettuce leaves. Top with yogurt, then a sprinkle of shredded cheese.

CONTINENTAL PEAR SALAD

1 (1 pound, 13 ounce) can pear halves
1 (5 ounce) jar Old English cheese
1 (3 ounce) package cream cheese
2 tablespoons pear syrup
1/4 cup chopped dates
1/4 cup chopped cashew nuts
Lettuce
Cashew nuts for garnish

Chill pears. Bring cheeses to room temperature. Drain chilled pears and reserve 2 tablespoons syrup. Place pear halves, cut-side-up on a lettuce lined platter or on individual salad plates. Combine cheeses, thinning a little with reserved pear syrup. Blend in the chopped dates and cashews. Carefully place a spoonful of cheese mixture in each pear half. Top each serving with a cashew nut. Makes 4 to 6 servings.

SLIGHTLY ANCHOVY PEAR SALAD

3 large fresh pears
1/3 cup soft processed cheese
4 tablespoons cream cheese
1 1/3 tablespoons anchovy paste
1/3 teaspoon milk
2/3 teaspoon lemon juice
Lettuce leaves
French dressing

Pare, core and slice pears. Arrange on lettuce leaves. Mix cheeses, anchovy paste, milk and lemon juice. Spoon over pears. Serve with French dressing. Serves 6.

PEAR CRUNCH SALAD

6 ripe pears
6 teaspoons lemon juice
1/2 cup chopped walnuts
1/4 cup chopped ripe olives
1/2 cup mayonnaise
Crisp salad greens

Core pears and trim tops to give petal shape. Sprinkle 1 teaspoon lemon juice over each pear. Combine celery, walnuts, olives and mayonnaise. Fill the pears with the crunchy mixture. Serve on individual salad plates lined with salad greens. Makes 6 salads.

PEAR CHEF SALAD

Salad greens
2 fresh pears
1 cup julienne strips cooked ham
1 cup julienne strips cooked chicken
1 cup julienne strips cheddar cheese
1 small cucumber, scored and sliced
Radish roses for garnish
Dressing

Place torn greens in shallow salad bowl or deep platter. Cut pears into wedges and core. Arrange pears, ham, chicken, cheese and cucumber slices over greens. Garnish with radish roses. Serve with Tarragon dressing.

Tarragon Dressing

1 cup mayonnaise
2 tablespoons tarragon vinegar
1 teaspoon lemon juice
2 teaspoons catsup
1 teaspoon sugar
1/2 teaspoon tarragon

Combine all ingredients and mix until smooth; chill.

LIGHT-STYLE BARTLETT SALAD

4 or 5 frilly lettuce leaves
8 cups lettuce, chopped (1 to 2 heads)
Light-Style Green Goddess Dressing
2 eggs, hard-cooked, shelled
4 slices bacon, cooked, drained, crumbled
2 fresh Bartlett pears, cored and cubed
3/4 cup chopped ripe tomato
1/4 cup chopped green onion

Line plate or shallow bowl with frilly lettuce leaves. Toss chopped lettuce with half the dressing in another bowl. Turn onto lettuce-lined bowl. Halve eggs and separate yolks from whites. Chop yolks and whites separately. Arrange separate rows of egg yolks, whites, bacon, pear cubes, tomato and onion on top of salad. Serve the remaining dressing separately. Makes 4 servings.

Light Style Green Goddess Dressing

Combine in blender 1/3 cup parsley leaves, 2 tablespoons white vinegar, 2 cloves garlic, 1 tablespoon sugar, 2 teaspoons dried tarragon, 1/2 teaspoon salt. Whirl until finely pureed. Stir (don't use blender) into 2 cups plain yogurt.

PEAR SALAD WITH CORIANDER DRESSING

2 cans (16 ounces each) pear halves
1 orange, peeled and sliced
1/2 cup thinly sliced red onion rings
1/2 cup thinly sliced green pepper rings

Drain pears; reserve 1/4 cup syrup for use in dressing. Halve each orange slice. Gently toss all ingredients. Refrigerate at least 1 hour. Garnish with fresh parsley. Serve with Coriander dressing. Serves 6 to 8.

Coriander Dressing

Combine 1/4 cup salad oil, 1/4 cup white wine vinegar and 1/4 cup reserved pear syrup. Add 1 tablespoon lime juice, 1 teaspoon salt, 1/4 teaspoon ground coriander, 1/4 teaspoon grated lime peel, and 1/4 teaspoon bottled hot pepper sauce. Mix well. Makes 3/4 cup dressing.

FRESH PEAR PLATTER SALAD

2 fresh Anjou pears
1 apple
2 oranges
1/4 cup sugar
Salad greens
1/2 teaspoon salt
1 1g. bunch seedless grapes
1/2 teaspoon dry mustard
1/2 teaspoon paprika
1/2 teaspoon celery seed
1 tablespoon vinegar
 2 tablespoons lemon juice
 1/2 cup salad oil

Core and quarter pears. Core and cut apple into wedges. Peel and slice oranges. Arrange fruits on platter lined with salad greens. Combine salt, sugar, mustard, paprika, celery seed, vinegar and lemon juice. Mix into a paste. Gradually add oil, blending well. Serve drizzled over fresh fruits. Makes 6 servings.

PEAR-MACAROON SALAD

1 can pears, drained
1 (3 ounce) package cream cheese
2 tablespoons mayonnaise
Macaroon cookies, crumbled
Maraschino cherries
Lettuce

Blend cheese and mayonnaise together. Spread each pear half with cream cheese mixture. Sprinkle crumbled macaroons on each pear half. Top each with a maraschino cherry. Serve on platter lined with fresh lettuce leaves or on individual salad plates lined with lettuce.

SIX SLIM GIRLS' SALAD

3 fresh pears
1 cup fresh pineapple chunks
1 cup cantaloupe balls
1/2 cup seedless grapes
1/4 cup lemon juice
1/2 teaspoon non-caloric liquid sweetener
1/4 teaspoon peppermint extract
1/2 teaspoon dried peppermint
1 pint raspberry sherbet

Pare, halve and core pears; cut into lengthwise slices. Combine pears, pineapple, cantaloupe and grapes in bowl. Mix lemon juice, sweetener and peppermint extract; toss with fruit. Chill. To serve, place fruit in ring on serving plate; sprinkle with dried peppermint. Scoop sherbet into center. Makes 6 servings.

WESTERN PEAR SALAD

8 canned pear halves
2 cups cottage cheese
1/2 cup finely chopped celery
1/4 cup finely chopped green pepper
1/4 teaspoon salt
2 teaspoons grated orange peel
8 orange slices
Lettuce
French dressing

Drain pears and arrange on plates with orange slices. Combine cottage cheese, celery, green pepper, salt and orange peel. Mound onto pears. Use French dressing of your choice. Serves 6.

PEAR MELBA SALAD

3 ripe Western winter pears
Lemon juice
Crisp lettuce
1 (3 ounce) package cream cheese
1/4 cup chopped walnuts
1 (10-ounce) package frozen raspberries
1/4 cup sugar
1 tablespoon corn starch
1/4 cup port wine

Halve and core Anjou, Bosc, or Comice pears. Brush cut sides with lemon juice. Place pear halves on lettuce lined platter. Divide cream cheese into 6 portions and shape into balls. Roll in chopped walnuts and place cheese balls in centers of pears. Thaw and blend raspberries in blender or put through sieve. Combine sugar, raspberries, corn starch and wine in saucepan. Bring to boil. Cook over medium heat, stirring frequently until sauce is thickened and clear. Chill. Serve sauce over stuffed pears. Makes 6 servings.

PEANUT BUTTER AND JELLY SALAD

1/2 cup peanut butter, chunk style
1/2 cup dairy sour cream
2 fresh pears
2 oranges
1 quart chopped iceberg lettuce
6 teaspoon red jelly or jam

Beat peanut butter with sour cream until smooth. Pare, core and slice pears. Peel oranges, slice then cut slices in half. Toss pears, oranges and lettuce. Put into 6 individual salad bowls. Spoon some peanut butter dressing onto each salad and top with jelly. Chill. Serves 6.

HOT SPICED FRUIT SALAD

1 can (1 pound each) peach halves, pineapple chunks, pitted light sweet cherries, pear halves and apricot halves, drained, reserving liquid
2 tart apples
3 tablespoons lemon juice
1/2 teaspoon ground nutmeg
1/2 teaspoon ground cinnamon
1/4 teaspoon ground cloves
1/3 cup firmly packed brown sugar
1/4 cup butter
3 bananas
2 cups seedless grapes
Sour cream, whipped cream, or unflavored yogurt

Drain and combine syrup from fruits. Reserve 1 1/2 cups combined fruit syrup. Core and dice apple: mix with lemon juice. Turn all drained fruits and apples into a 2 1/2 quart baking dish. Stir together fruit syrup, nutmeg, cinnamon, cloves and brown sugar. Pour over fruit. Dot with butter. Cover and bake in 350-degree oven for 20 minutes. Peel banana and cut into chunks. Lightly stir grapes and bananas into baked fruit, and cover and bake for 5 more minutes. Serve hot with sour cream, whipped cream or unflavored yogurt. Makes 12 servings.

PEAR WALDORF SALAD

3 fresh winter pears
1 can (8 3/4 ounce) pineapple chunks, drained
1/2 cup sliced celery
1 can (8 ounce) mandarin oranges, drained
1/4 cup slivered almonds, toasted
3/4 cup mayonnaise
1 tablespoon chopped candied ginger
2 tablespoons pineapple syrup
1 teaspoon grated lemon peel

Reserve and slice 1/2 pear for garnish. Core and dice remaining pears. Place diced pears in salad bowl with the pineapple, celery, mandarin oranges and almonds. Combine mayonnaise, ginger, pineapple syrup and lemon peel. Add to pear mixture and toss lightly. Garnish with reserved pear slices. Makes 5 to 6 servings.

41

PEAR AMBROSIA SALAD

3 fresh Bartlett pears
Lemon juice
1 can (8 ounce) crushed pineapple
2 egg yolks, beaten
2 tablespoons sugar
1 tablespoon vinegar
Dash salt
3 cups miniature marshmallows
1 cup chopped apple
1 can mandarin oranges, drained (11 ounce)
1/2 cup heavy cream, whipped (or use whipped topping)
 Sliced almonds

Drain pineapple, reserving syrup for dressing. In saucepan, combine 3
tablespoons of reserved pineapple syrup, egg yolks, sugar, vinegar and
salt. Cook, stirring until mixture thickens. Set aside to cool. Combine
marshmallows, apples, oranges and pineapple. Pour cooked dressing
over fruit and mix well. Fold in whipped cream. Refrigerate several
hours or overnight. Halve and core pears. Brush cut sides with lemon
juice. Spoon salad mixture into centers of pear halves. Sprinkle with
slivered almonds. Makes 6 salads.

FRESH FRUIT KABOBS

3 fresh ripe pears
3 bananas, peeled
1/2 cantaloupe
1 pint strawberries
Lemon juice

Core and slice each pear into 8 wedges. Slice each banana in eight chunks. Sprinkle the cut surfaces with lemon juice to prevent fruit form discoloring. On wooden skewers thread fruit to contrast in shape and color. Chill before serving. Drizzle Lemon-Lime Fruit Sauce over kabobs. Makes 12 kabobs.

Lemon-Lime Fruit Sauce

1/2 cup sour cream
1/2 cup plain yogurt
1/4 cup sifted powdered sugar
2 tablespoons freshly squeezed lemon juice 2 tablespoons freshly squeezed lime juice
1/2 teaspoon each grated lemon and lime peel
Combine all ingredients and mix well. Chill. Serve over fruit salad. Makes 1 cup dressing.

BASIC FRUIT DRESSING

2 tablespoons lemon or lime juice
2 tablespoons sugar or honey
Dash salt
1 cup sour cream

Blend juice, sugar or honey and salt; gradually blend in sour cream and refrigerate several hours to blend flavors. Makes about 1 1/4 cups dressing.

ORANGE HONEY DRESSING

1/4 cup mayonnaise
2 tablespoons honey
1 tablespoon freshly grated orange peel
Dash paprika

In bowl, combine all ingredients. Blend thoroughly. Makes about 1/3
cup dressing.

FRESH ORANGE FRUIT SALAD DRESSING

1/2 cup fresh orange juice
1 tablespoon fresh lemon juice
Dash salt
2 eggs, separated
6 tablespoons sugar
1/4 cup heavy cream, whipped
Grated orange rind for garnish

Heat orange juice over low heat. Beat lemon juice, salt and egg yolks
together in top of double boiler. Gradually beat in 4 tablespoons sugar,
slowly stir in hot orange juice. Cook over hot water until thickened,
stirring constantly. Beat egg whites until soft peaks form. Gradually
beat in remaining 2 tablespoons sugar. Fold into cooked mixture. Chill.
Fold in whipped cream just before serving. Makes 2 1/2 cups. Garnish
with grated orange rind if desired.

FRESH ORANGE FRUIT SALAD DRESSING

1/2 cup fresh orange juice
1 tablespoon fresh lemon juice
Dash salt
2 eggs, separated
6 tablespoons sugar
1/4 cup heavy cream, whipped
Grated orange rind for garnish

Heat orange juice over low heat. Beat lemon juice, salt and egg yolks together in top of double boiler. Gradually beat in 4 tablespoons sugar, slowly stir in hot orange juice. Cook over hot water until thickened, stirring constantly. Beat egg whites until soft peaks form. Gradually beat in remaining 2 tablespoons sugar. Fold into cooked mixture. Chill. Fold in whipped cream just before serving. Makes 2 1/2 cups. Garnish with grated orange rind if desired.

BASIC FRUIT DRESSING

2 tablespoons lemon or lime juice
2 tablespoons sugar or honey
Dash salt
1 cup sour cream
Blend juice, sugar or honey and salt; gradually blend in sour cream and refrigerate several hours to blend flavors. Makes about 1 1/4 cups dressing.

MAIN DISHES

HAM AND PEARS WITH BARBECUE SAUCE

1/4 cup chili sauce
1/4 cup catsup
1 tablespoon prepared horseradish
2 tablespoons melted butter
3 fresh pears
Lemon juice
1 center-cut ham slice (buy ready-to-eat) 1 1/2 pound, about 1 inch thick

Mix first 4 ingredients. Cut pears in quarters lengthwise; core and pare. Coat with lemon juice. Heat broiler. Place ham and pears on rack in pan. Brush pears with sauce. Broil 5 inches from heat until ham is lightly browned. Turn ham; brush pears with more sauce. Broil 3 minutes. Brush both ham and pears with sauce. Broil 2 to 3 minutes. Makes 6 servings.

SPICY GLAZED HAM LOAF AND PEARS

1 (29 ounce) can pear halves
1 1/2 pounds ground ham
1 pound fresh ground pork
1 cup soft bread crumbs
1 cup milk
2 eggs, slightly beaten
2 tablespoons vinegar
1 teaspoon dry mustard
1/2 cup orange marmalade
1/4 cup brown sugar
1/8 teaspoon cloves
1/8 teaspoon allspice
Parsley, for garnish

Drain pears, reserving 1/2 cup syrup. Combine ham, pork, bread crumbs, milk and eggs. Mix well. Add vinegar and mustard. Blend thoroughly. Shape into loaf and place in baking pan. Bake at 350 degrees for 1 hour. Meanwhile in small saucepan combine reserved 1/2 cup syrup, orange marmalade, brown sugar, spices and prepared mustard. Bring to a boil and cook for 5 minutes. Place pear halves around ham loaf and spoon glaze over pears and ham. Return to oven and bake for another 30 minutes, basting occasionally with glaze. Serve ham loaf on platter surrounded by pear halves. Garnish with fresh parsley. Serves 6 to 8.

HAM WITH PEARS APRICOTINE

Cooked center-cut ham slice
Whole cloves
2 fresh pears
3/4 cup apricot jam

Stud edge of ham with cloves. Place in baking dish. Heat in 375-degree oven for 20 minutes. Pare, halve and core pears. Cut into slices. Place on ham and spoon jam over all. Heat 10 minutes longer and serve hot.

ROSY BAKED PEARS AND HAM

3 fresh pears
1 cup canned whole berry cranberry sauce
1 teaspoon grated orange rind
1/4 cup orange juice
2 tablespoons melted butter
1/4 cup roasted diced almonds
Baked ham

Pare, halve and core pears; place cut sides up in baking dish. Mix together all remaining ingredients except ham; spoon into pear halves, pouring liquid over and around pears. Cover dish tightly and bake in 350-degree oven 30 to 35 minutes. Serve warm as accompaniment for baked ham. Makes 6 servings.

PEARS AND PORK CHOPS

1 (16 ounce) can pear halves
6 pork chops
1/2 cup white wine
2 tablespoons cider vinegar
2 tablespoons brown sugar
12 dried apricots

Drain pear halves, reserving syrup. In skillet, brown pork chops. Add
pear syrup, wine, vinegar, sugar and apricots. Cover and simmer for 45
minutes. Arrange pear halves on pork chops and spoon sauce over
pears and meat. Cover and simmer 15 more minutes, glazing
occasionally.
Serves 6

BACON AND PEAR STEW

1 pound dried pears
1 1/2 cups hot water
1/4 pound smoked bacon
2 1/4 pound's potatoes, sliced thickly
Salt and pepper to taste
1/2 cup cream

Pour boiling water over pears and leave for several hours or overnight.
Cut bacon into cubes and fry in a large pan for 2 to 3 minutes, then add
the pears and the water in which they were soaked. Cover and simmer
for 30 minutes. Add potatoes, season to taste and continue cooking
until potatoes are tender. Add cream and serve. Serves 4 to 6

SPICED PORK ROAST WITH PEARS

4 to 4 1/2 pound bone-in pork loin roast
1 clove garlic, halved
1/2 teaspoon salt
1/4 teaspoon pepper
3/4 teaspoon ginger
3/4 teaspoon cinnamon
1/4 cup firmly packed brown sugar
2 tablespoons lemon juice
1/2 cup dry sherry or apple juice
3 or 4 ripe Anjou pears
1 tablespoon cornstarch mixed with 2 tablespoons water

Place roast, fat side up, on rack in roasting pan. Rub meat with garlic, then drop garlic in pan. Insert a neat thermometer into thickest part of meat, without touching bone. Roast uncovered in 325-degree oven for one and half hours until thermometer reaches 140 degrees. Meanwhile in small bowl, stir salt, pepper, ginger, cinnamon, sugar, lemon juice and sherry. Peel, quarter and core pears. When roast reaches 140 degrees, remove roast and rack from pan. Place meat directly in pan, add pears and pour sherry mixture over roast and pears. Return to oven and continue roasting for 45 minutes or until thermometer reads 170 degrees. Baste often with pan drippings. Remove pork and pears to platter. Skim fat from drippings. Pour drippings into pan, scraping browned particles free from roasting pan. Stir cornstarch mixture into drippings and cook over medium heat, stirring, until sauce boils and thickens. Serve with pork. Makes 6 to 8 servings.

CHICKEN SUPPER SOUP

2 cans (10 3/4 ounce) condensed chicken broth
2 half breast of chicken
1 cup diced raw potato
1 cup julienne-cut carrot
1/2 cup chopped onion
1 small clove fresh garlic, minced
1 teaspoon salt
1/2 bay leaf
2 medium size fresh ripe pears
1 large tomato
2 cups water
1 cup whole kernel corn (fresh, frozen or canned)
1 cup sliced zucchini
1/2 cup chopped celery
1 tablespoon wine vinegar
1/4 teaspoon white pepper
1/16 teaspoon nutmeg
2 thin slices lemon
Parmesan cheese

Combine chicken broth, chicken, potato, carrot, onion, garlic, salt and bay leaf in 4 quart kettle. Bring to boil, cover and cook over low heat for 15 minutes. Remove chicken and cool. Remove skin and bones and shred meat. Return chicken meat to soup kettle. Pare, core, and dice pears. Peel, seed and dice tomato. Add pears, tomatoes, water and all remaining ingredients, except parmesan cheese in soup kettle. Bring to a boil and cook 5 minutes until vegetables are tender. Skim off and discard any surface fat. Ladle soup into serving bowls and sprinkle with cheese. Serves 5

ORIENTAL PEAR AND CHICKEN SAUTE

2 whole chicken breasts
2 tablespoons oil
2 winter pears, cored and sliced
1 package (10 ounce) frozen pea pods, thawed
1 can (6 ounce) sliced bamboo shoots, drained
1/2 cup diagonally sliced celery
3 green onions, cut into 1/2 inch pieces
1 tablespoon cornstarch
1 teaspoon sugar
1/2 teaspoon salt
1 cup chicken stock
3 tablespoons soy sauce
1/2 cup cashew nuts

Remove skin and bones from chicken. Cut into 3/4 inch cubes. In a skillet or wok, stir-fry chicken in hot oil 2 minutes. Add pears, pea pods, bamboo shoots, celery and green onions. Stir-fry 2 minutes. Combine cornstarch sugar, salt, chicken stock and soy sauce. Add to skillet. Cook and stir until thickened. Simmer, covered 2 to 3 minutes. Garnish with cashew nuts before serving. Makes 6 servings.

FRUIT-SAUCED CHICKEN

1/2 cup flour
1/2 teaspoon salt
Dash pepper
1 frying chicken cut up (3 to 3 1/2 pounds.)
1/2 cup shortening
1/3 cup orange juice
2 tablespoons water
1 teaspoon vinegar
1/2 teaspoon grated orange rind
1/2 teaspoon powdered ginger
1 1/2 cups sliced fresh pears
1 cup sliced fresh nectarines

Combine flour, salt and pepper; coat chicken with seasoned flour.
Brown very slowly in hot shortening. Pour off excess fat; add orange
juice, water and vinegar. Sprinkle with orange rind and ginger. Cover;
cook 10 to 15 minutes. Remove chicken from pan; Keep warm.
Thicken sauce slightly with 1 teaspoon cornstarch. Add pears and
nectarines to sauce and heat through. Spoon over chicken. Makes 5
servings.

LEMON CHICKEN WITH PEARS

3 tablespoons oil
1 chicken breast, skinned, boned and cut in 1 inch cubes
1/2 pound Chinese pea pods or green beans
3 green onions, green part only, cut into 1-inch lengths
2 fresh pears, cored, sliced
Cooking sauce

Heat 2 tablespoons oil in wok or large skillet. Add chicken cubes and
stir fry over high heat for 2 minutes. Transfer chicken to plate. Add
remaining oil and stir-fry peas 1 minute over high heat. Reduce heat to
medium. Add cooked chicken, onions, pears and cooking sauce. Stir-fry
until mixture is heated through and sauce is glossy, about 3 minutes.
Makes 2 or 3 servings.

Cooking Sauce

Combine 3 tablespoons water, 2 tablespoons soy sauce, 1 teaspoon
grated lemon peel, 2 tablespoons lemon juice, 2 cloves minced garlic, 2
teaspoons sugar, 2 teaspoons cornstarch and 2 teaspoons ginger
(minced or grated) in small cup.

CURRIED PEARS WITH LAMB

1 can pear halves, or 3 fresh pears
6 lamb chops
1/4 cup brown sugar
2 teaspoons grated orange peel
1 teaspoon curry powder
2 tablespoons butter

Broil lamb chops and turn. Drain pears and place on broiler pan. Fill with sugar, orange peel, curry powder, and butter. Broil until pears are heated and lamb chops reach desired doneness. Serves 6

HEAVEN & EARTH

4 medium potatoes
6 bacon strips
2 medium onions, thinly sliced
4 fresh pears, peeled and sliced
1 tablespoon sugar
1/4 cup cider vinegar
1 teaspoon nutmeg
1/4 cup minced parsley
1/2 teaspoon salt
1/2 teaspoon pepper

Cook potatoes in boiling water 35 to 40 minutes or until tender. Let cool slightly, peel and dice into 1-inch squares. Fry bacon in medium skillet until tender and crispy. Remove and drain on paper towels. Crumble bacon, reserving 2 strips for topping. Sauté onions in remaining bacon drippings until tender. Combine all ingredients in a 2-quart casserole dish. Bake in 375-degree oven for 20 minutes, till heated through. Garnish with reserved bacon strips and parsley sprigs and tomato wedges. Makes 4 to 6 servings.

PEAR CORNED BEEF HASH

2 fresh ripe pears
2 tablespoons oil
1 cup diced cooked potato
1 cup chopped onion
1/2 cup shredded carrot
2 tablespoons Worcestershire sauce
2 tablespoons prepared mustard
1/2 teaspoon dried basil, crumbled
1/4 teaspoon dried dill weed
2 cups coarsely chopped cooked corned beef **
1/4 cup milk **
Salt to taste
1 small tomato

Core and dice about 1 or 2 pears to make 1 1/2 cups. Reserve remaining pear for garnish. Heat oil in 9-inch skillet, add potato, onion and carrot. Sauté 2 minutes, or until onion is transparent. Mix Worcestershire sauce, mustard, basil and dill together. Add to vegetables in skillet. Stir in corned beef, diced pear and milk. Sprinkle salt to taste. Cook 5 to 10 minutes, until heated through. Serve hot, garnished with remaining pear and tomato cut into wedges. Makes 4 servings.

**May use 1 (15 ounce) can corned beef hash and omit the milk.

BAVARIAN MEATBALLS AND PEARS

1 (29 ounce) can pear halves
1 1/2 pounds ground beef
1/4 cup bread crumbs
1/4 cup evaporated milk
1/3 cup minced onion
1 egg
1 teaspoon salt
1/4 teaspoon pepper
2 tablespoons vegetable oil
1 cup plus
2 tablespoons pear syrup
1/4 cup cider vinegar
2 cloves
1 bay leaf
1 tablespoon all-purpose flour

Drain pear halves, reserving syrup. Combine ground beef bread crumbs, milk, egg, onion, salt and pepper. Mix well. Shape into 2-inch meatballs and brown slowly in oil. Add 1 cup pear syrup, vinegar, cloves and bay leaf. Cover and simmer 25 minutes. Add pear halves; simmer 10 minutes longer, or until meat is done. Remove meat and pears to platter; keep warm. Mix flour with 2 tablespoons pear syrup. Slowly stir into skillet juices and cook until thickened. Pour over meat and pears. Makes 4 to 6 servings.

FRANCISCAN POT ROAST

1 beef pot roast
2 cups water
3/4 cup red wine
1/2 crushed bay leaf
8 sliced carrots
4 or 5 pears
whole cloves
1/3 cup catsup or chili sauce
2 tablespoons cornstarch
2 tablespoons water salt and pepper

Brown meat. Mix water, wine, catsup and bay leaf, pour over meat. Simmer 2 to 2 1/2 hours. Add carrots, cook for another 30 minutes. Pare and halve pears, stud each half with 3 cloves. Remove meat and carrots to platter; keep warm. Skim fat from stock. Add pears, cook 6 to 8 minutes. Mix cornstarch and water. Stir into sauce, cook until thickened. Arrange pears on platter with beef and carrots. Serve with sauce. Cooking time may vary, depending on size of pot roast.

SAUSAGE-STUFFED PEARS

1/2 lb. bulk pork sausage
1/2 cup chopped onion
1/4 cup sliced celery
1/4 teaspoon salt
1/4 teaspoon ground sage
1/4 teaspoon dry mustard
1/2 cup soft bread crumbs
2 large fresh ripe pears
1/4 cup water

Brown sausage with onion and celery. Stir in salt, sage, mustard and bread crumbs. Halve pears and core. Cut a very thin slice off rounded side of each pear half, so pears sit level and arrange in 9-inch pie pan. Heap stuffing over pears. Pour water into pan, bake in 350-degree oven for 30 minutes, until pears are tender.

BEANS & PEARS

For lunch in a hurry, spoon canned baked beans into halves of fresh Bartlett pears, which have been cored. Drizzle with catsup and top with grated cheddar cheese. Bake at 350 degrees until heated, about 20 minutes.

LIMAS AND PEARS

6 cups frozen Baby Lima beans, defrosted
6 cups pears, peeled, cored and sliced
1/2 cup molasses
1/2 cup chicken stock
1/2 cup chopped onion
Place all ingredients into a crock-pot. Mix together. Cover and cook on High all day, at least 8 hours.

BAKED TUNA STUFFED PEARS

2 medium size ripe pears
2 teaspoons lemon juice
1 can (7 ounce) solid pack white tuna
3/4 cup shredded sharp cheddar cheese
1/2 cup thinly sliced celery
1/4 cup sliced green onion
2 tablespoons sliced pimiento
1/4 cup mayonnaise
2 teaspoons grated parmesan cheese

Cut pears into half, lengthwise and remove cores. Cut a thin slice from rounded side of each so pears will sit level; then place in shallow baking pan. Brush cut surfaces with lemon juice. Drain tuna, break into chunks and mix with 1/2 cup of the cheddar cheese, celery, onion, pimento and mayonnaise. Top each pear half with 1/2 cup tuna mixture. Sprinkle tops with remaining cheddar cheese and parmesan cheese. Pour 1/4 cup water into pan around pears. Bake at 350 degrees for about 25 minutes, or just until pears are tender but not mushy. Serve hot. Makes 4 servings.

STIR-FRY ZUCCHINI AND PEARS

2 medium fresh ripe pears
3 cups thinly sliced zucchini
1/2 cup thinly sliced onion
1 tablespoon olive oil
1 small clove fresh garlic, pressed
1/2 teaspoon salt
1/4 teaspoon oregano
1/4 teaspoon basil
1/4 teaspoon grated lemon peel
1/4 cup grated parmesan cheese

Select firm-ripe pears, remove cores and cut fruit in 1/4-inch pieces to measure 2 cups. Slice zucchini about 1/8 inch thick and prepare onion. Heat oil in 10-inch skillet and stir in garlic, salt and herbs. Add zucchini, onion and lemon peel and stir-fry over moderate heat about 5 minutes, just until zucchini is tender. Add pears and mix gently. Sprinkle with cheese. Cover skillet and steam for 5 minutes, until pears are thoroughly heated. Serve at once. Makes 4 servings.

PEAR FAIR PIZZA

Heat oven to 450 degrees
Grease 12-inch pizza pan
Cooking time 15 to 20 minutes

DOUGH

2 1/2 cups Bisquick Mix
1/2 cup plus 2 tablespoons water
2 tablespoons soft butter
1/2 cup sugar
1 teaspoon nutmeg

TOPPING

3 ripe, firm pears cut into 24 wedges (pear slicer works well)
1/2 cup chopped walnuts
3 tablespoons granulated sugar
1 teaspoon cinnamon
1/3 cup jam or jelly, any flavor
1 maraschino cherry

In mixing bowl, stir Bisquick, nutmeg, sugar, butter and water into soft ball of dough. Place ball of dough in center of pan and spread out to the edges. Arrange pear wedges into dough sideways in circular design. Scatter chopped walnuts among dough and pear wedges. Sprinkle sugar and cinnamon over pears, walnuts and dough. Place in preheated oven to bake. After removing from oven, add jam or jelly at random among pear wedges and dough. Place maraschino cherry in center. Serve warm or cold.

BAKED GOODS

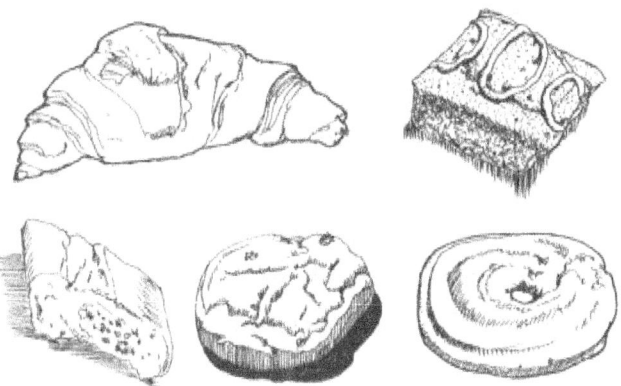

GINGERBREAD PEAR MUFFINS

1 medium pear
1 teaspoon lemon juice
2 cups all-purpose flour
1/2 cup firmly packed brown sugar
2 teaspoons ground ginger
1/2 teaspoon allspice
1 teaspoon baking soda
1/3 cup buttermilk
1/2 cup molasses
1/4 cup vegetable oil
2 eggs, slightly beaten

Peel, core and finely chop pear. Sprinkle lemon juice over pear in a
small bowl; toss well and set aside. Combine flour, brown sugar, ginger,
allspice, mixing well. Make a well in center of mixture. Dissolve soda in
buttermilk; stir in molasses, oil, eggs and pear mixture. Add to dry
ingredients, mixing till just moistened. Spoon batter into greased muffin
pans, filling 2/3 full. Bake at 350 degrees for 15 to 20 minutes. Yield,
20 muffins.

PEAR SCONES

1 ripe pear, peeled, cored and cut into pieces
1/2 teaspoon fresh lemon juice
2 cups all-purpose flour
1 tablespoon sugar
1 tablespoon double acting baking powder
1/2 teaspoon baking soda
1/2 teaspoon salt
3/4 stick (6 tablespoons) cold unsalted butter cut into bits
3 to 6 tablespoons buttermilk
Egg wash made by beating 1 large egg with 1 teaspoon water

Puree the pear and lemon juice in food processor or blender until smooth. Sift together flour, sugar, baking powder, baking soda and salt. Add butter and blend until the mixture resembles coarse cornmeal. In a small bowl beat the pear puree and 3 tablespoons of the buttermilk until mixture is combined well. Add pear and buttermilk mixture to the sifted flour mixture. Stir with a fork, adding more of the buttermilk if necessary until it just forms a sticky but manageable dough. Knead the dough lightly on a floured surface for 30 seconds and pat it gently into a round 1 inch thick. Cut out rounds with a 2-inch cutter dipped in flour and arrange the scones in a buttered baking sheet. Form the scraps into a ball, pat the dough into a round 1-inch thick and cut out scones in the same manner. Brush the tops of the scones with the egg wash and bake in preheated 425-degree oven for 12 to 15 minutes until lightly browned. Makes about 12 two inch scones.

PEAR MUFFINS

1/2 cup salad oil
2 cups sugar
3 eggs
3 cups flour
2 cups chopped pears, canned or fresh
1 teaspoon salt
1 teaspoon baking soda
1 teaspoon cinnamon
1/2 teaspoon cloves
1 teaspoon vanilla

Put oil, sugar and egg into a bowl, beat well. Sift together flour, salt, soda, cinnamon and cloves. Add to creamed mixture. Add vanilla. Fold in pears. Divide into 30 greased muffin cups. Bake at 350 degrees for 20 to 25 minutes until golden brown.

SPICED PEAR BREAD

1/2 cup butter
2 teaspoons baking powder
1 cup sugar
2 cinnamon
2 eggs
1 teaspoon salt
1 pound ripe pears, peeled, cored, chopped (2 cups)
1/2 teaspoon cloves
2 1/2 cups flour
1/2 teaspoon nutmeg

Cream butter and sugar. Beat in eggs and pear. Sift dry ingredients; blend into pear mixture. Turn into greased 9-inch loaf pan. Bake at 350 degrees 1 hour to 1 hour and 15 minutes, or until pick inserted in center comes out clean. Cool slightly; turn out onto wire rack. Makes 1 loaf.

LEMON PEAR NUT BREAD

1/2 cup butter
1 teaspoon nutmeg
1/2 cup brown sugar
2 teaspoons grated lemon peel
1/2 cup sugar
2 cups chopped pears
1 egg
2/3 cup chopped walnuts
2 cups flour
1/2 teaspoon salt
1 teaspoon baking soda

Cream together butter and sugars. Add egg. Sift dry ingredients and add to sugar mixture. Stir in pears
and nuts. Bake at 350 degrees for 55 minutes in 3 small greased loaf pans.

Lemon Glaze: 1/2 cup lemon juice, 1/2 cup sugar Combine till sugar is dissolved, pour over warm loaves. Cool before removing from pans.

QUICK PEAR BREAD

1/2 cup shortening
1/2 teaspoon allspice
1/2 cup brown sugar
1 teaspoon cinnamon
1/2 cup sugar
1/2 teaspoon salt
1 egg
2 cups pears, cored, chopped
2 cups flour
1 teaspoon baking soda
2/3 cup chopped walnuts

Cream together shortening, and sugars. Add egg, beat. Sift together flour, soda, allspice, cinnamon and salt. Add to creamed mixture, stir in pears and nuts. Pour into a 9-inch greased loaf pan. Bake at 350 degrees for 1 hour. Let stand until cool. Remove bread from pan. Dust with powdered sugar, if desired. Makes 1 loaf.

PICNIC PEAR NUT BREAD

2 fresh ripe pears
2 large eggs, beaten
1 cup whole bran
1 1/2 cups sifted all-purpose flour
1/2 cup sugar
1 teaspoon baking powder
1/2 teaspoon salt
1/2 teaspoon baking soda
1/4 cup soft shortening
1/2 cup chopped walnuts

Core and finely chop unpeeled pears to measure 1 1/4 cups. Combine with eggs and bran; let stand while preparing remaining ingredients. Resift flour with sugar, baking powder, salt and soda into mixing bowl. Add shortening and pear-bran mixture; mix until all the flour is moistened. Stir in walnuts. Turn into a well-greased 8 1/2 x 4 1/2 x 2 1/2-inch loaf pan. Let stand 20 minutes. Bake below oven center in 350-degree oven for 1 to 1 1/4 hours, until pick inserted in center comes out clean. Let stand 10 minutes, then turn out onto wire rack to cool. Serve with Lemon-Mint butter.
** Spiced variation; add 1/2 teaspoon ginger and 1/4 teaspoon nutmeg to flour mixture.

Lemon Mint Butter

Beat 1 cup softened butter with 1 teaspoon grated lemon peel and 2 tablespoons chopped fresh mint leaves. Makes 1 cup butter.

ORANGE-GLAZED PEAR NUT BREAD

1 can (16 ounce.) pear halves
1 1/2 cups all-purpose flour
 3/4 cup sugar
1 tablespoon baking powder
1 teaspoon salt
1/4 teaspoon allspice
1 cup whole wheat flour
1/4 cup oil
1 egg, beaten
1 tablespoon orange rind
1 cup chopped walnuts

Drain pears, reserving syrup. Reserve 1 pear half for garnish. Puree remaining pears. Add reserved pear syrup to pureed pears to equal 1 cup. Sift together flour, sugar, baking powder, salt and allspice. Stir in whole wheat flour. Mix pureed pears with oil, egg and orange rind. Stir into flour mixture and blend in nuts. Pour into greased 9 x 5-inch loaf pan. Slice pear half into sixths and place slices on batter. Bake at 350 degrees for 50 to 55 minutes. Spoon Orange Glaze over top of warm bread. Store overnight before slicing.

Orange Glaze
Blend 2 to 3 tablespoons orange juice into 1 cup powdered sugar to make a thin glaze.

SOUR CREAM PEAR NUT BREAD

1 cup pears chopped
2 cups sifted flour
1/2 cup oil
1/2 teaspoon salt
1 cup sugar
1 teaspoon soda
2 eggs
1/4 teaspoon cinnamon
1/4 cup sour cream
1/4 teaspoon nutmeg
1 teaspoon vanilla
1 cup chopped nuts

Peel, core and chop pears. In a large bowl beat oil and sugar till well blended. Beat in eggs, one at a time, sour cream and vanilla. Sift dry ingredients together. Add to creamed mixture and blend. Add pears and chopped nuts and mix. Divide batter into 3 small loaf pans which have been greased. Bake for 45 mm. at 350 degrees. Let cool in pan for 10 minutes. Remove from pan and continue to cool on wire rack.

PEAR ANADAMA BREAD

2 large fresh pears
1 tablespoon lemon juice
1/2 cup yellow cornmeal
1/4 cup butter
1/4 cup light molasses
1 1/2 teaspoon salt
1/4 teaspoon allspice
1 cake compressed yeast
3 1/4 cups flour
1 egg

Puree enough pear with lemon juice in electric blender to get 1 cup puree (1 to 1 1/2 pears). Turn into saucepan. Stir in all but 1 tablespoon cornmeal. Cook over medium-high heat, stirring constantly for 2 or 3 minutes until thickened. Remove from heat. Stir in butter until melted. Mix in molasses, salt and allspice. Cool to lukewarm (105-115 degrees). Crumble yeast into cornmeal mixture and stir until dissolved. Coarsely chop remaining pear. Mix into yeast mixture along with flour and egg to get a soft dough. Form into a 7-inch round mound. Place in greased and floured 8-inch cake pan. Sprinkle remaining 1 tablespoon cornmeal over top. Set in warm place for about 1 hour or until dough raises to top of pan. Bake in a 375-degree oven for 45 minutes or until baked through. Cover top loosely with foil after 30 minutes if top begins to get too brown. Makes 1 loaf.

PEAR PINWHEEL BREAD

2 or 3 fresh ripe pears
1/2 cup walnuts, chopped
1/2 cup sugar
1/2 teaspoon cinnamon
1/4 teaspoon nutmeg
2 1/3 cups biscuit mix
1/2 cup milk
1 egg beaten
2 tablespoons butter, melted
Powdered sugar

Core and chop unpeeled pears. Combine pears with walnuts, sugar, cinnamon, and nutmeg. Lightly mix together biscuit mix, milk, egg and butter. Roll out on floured board to rectangle about 13 x 9 inches. Spread pear mixture over surface within about 1/2 inch from edge. With a 9-inch side towards you, roll away from you, jelly roll style, to produce a 9-inch roll. Bake seam side down in greased loaf pan (9 x 5 x 3 inches) for 55 to 60 minutes in 350-degree oven. Cool; carefully remove from pan. Dust top with powdered sugar. Makes one loaf.

YOGURT-PEAR COFFEE CAKE

1 1/2 cups sifted all-purpose flour
2 teaspoons baking powder
1/4 teaspoon baking soda
3/4 teaspoon salt
2 medium-sized fresh pears
1 large egg
2/3 cup sugar
1/4 cup soft butter
1/2 teaspoon brandy extract
1/2 cup plain yogurt
Sugar-Crumb topping

Sift flour, baking powder, soda and salt. Cut pears in half. Finely chop about 1/2 pear to measure 1/2 cup. Cut remaining pear lengthwise into 16 slices. Beat egg until foamy. Beat in sugar, soft butter and brandy extract, beating until light and fluffy. Add yogurt and chopped pear; beat to blend. (Batter will appear curdled). Stir in flour mixture. Spoon into greased pan (7x11x1/2 inches). Arrange pear slices over top. Sprinkle with Sugar-Crumb mixture. Bake in moderate oven 375 degrees for 35 to 40 minutes, until cake tests done. Makes 8 servings.

Sugar-Crumb Topping

1/3 cup sugar
1/2 cup flour
1/2 teaspoon cinnamon
2 tablespoons butter
Mix flour, sugar and cinnamon together. Cut in butter to make crumbly mixture.

SPICY PEAR COFFEE CAKE

1 9-inch square spice cake
3 fresh ripe pears
1/3 cup sugar
1/3 cup water
2 tablespoons red cinnamon candies

Prepare and bake spice cake. Pare and slice pears. Combine sugar, water
and candies and heat until boiling; add pear slices. Simmer until tender.
Drain. Place pears on warm cake.

Combine:
6 tablespoons melted butter
3/4 cup brown sugar
1/3 cup chopped walnuts
2 tablespoons milk

Spoon over pears and cake, and broil

PEAR BERRY COFFEECAKE

3 fresh pears, peeled and cored
1 teaspoon lemon Juice
1 (13-ounce) package blueberry muffin mix
1/2 cup brown sugar
1/2 cup all-purpose flour
1/4 teaspoon nutmeg
1/4 cup butter

Prepare muffin mix using package directions. Put into greased 9-inch
square pan. Top with lemon-sprinkled pears sliced lengthwise into
eighths. Mix brown sugar, flour and nutmeg; cut in butter. Spoon
crumbly mixture over blueberry mix and pears. Bake at 400 degrees for
about 35 minutes. Good served slightly warm. Serves 10 to 12.

PEAR CRISP COFFEE CAKE

1 egg
3/4 cup dairy sour cream
1/4 cup granulated sugar
2 tablespoons melted butter
2 cups biscuit mix
2 fresh pears
2 tablespoons butter
1/3 cup packed brown sugar
1/4 cup flour
1 teaspoon allspice
1/2 teaspoon nutmeg
1/2 cup chopped walnuts

Cream together egg, sour cream, sugar, and melted butter. Add biscuit mix and beat for about 30 seconds. Spread in greased 8-inch baking dish. Halve, peel and core pears. Slice and place neatly over dough to cover it. Mix remaining ingredients until crumbly. Spread over pear. Bake at 400 degrees for about 30 minutes. Makes about 10 servings.

DESSERTS

DELTA PEAR CAKE

2 cups sugar
2 eggs
1/2 cup oil
4 cups firm pears, peeled and diced
2 cups flour
1 teaspoon cinnamon
1 teaspoon nutmeg
1/4 teaspoon cloves
1 teaspoon salt
2 teaspoons baking soda
1 cup chopped walnuts
1 cup raisins

Beat sugar, eggs and oil thoroughly for 2 minutes.
Add diced pears and mix. Sift together flour, cinnamon, nutmeg, cloves, salt and soda. Add to creamed mixture. Fold in chopped nuts and raisins. Turn into greased and floured 9 x 13-inch pan. Top with sprinkling of brown sugar and chopped nuts. Bake at 350 degrees for 1 hour. Serve hot or cold. Cake freezes well. Stores well fresh in refrigerator several days.

OLD-FASHIONED PEAR SPICE CAKE
WITH CREAM CHEESE FROSTING

1 1/2 cups sugar

1 1/2 cups salad oil

2 teaspoons baking powder

2 teaspoons baking soda

2 teaspoons ground cinnamon

1/2 teaspoon ground ginger

1/2 teaspoon salt

2 cups all-purpose flour

4 eggs

3 medium-size ripe pears

1/2 cup chopped walnuts or almonds

Combine the sugar, oil, baking powder, soda, cinnamon, ginger, salt, and flour. Beat on medium-high in mixer for 5 minutes. Beat in eggs, 1 at a time. Peel and core pears and cut into 1/2 inch chunks. By hand fold pears and nuts into batter. Spoon Into an ungreased 9 x 13-inch glass baking dish. Bake at 325 degrees for about 1 hour, until a wooden pick inserted into center comes out clean. Cool. Spread on frosting. Serves 12

Cream Cheese Frosting

Beat 1/4 cup soft butter, 1 (3 ounce) package cream cheese, softened, and 1 teaspoon vanilla until smooth. Beat in 2 1/2 cups sifted powdered sugar. Spread on cake.

PEAR BUNDT CAKE WITH ORANGE GLAZE

1 1/2 cups salad oil
2 cups sugar
3 eggs
3 cups sifted flour
1 teaspoon salt
1 teaspoon baking soda
1 teaspoon cinnamon
1 teaspoon vanilla
2 cups chopped ripe pears
1 cup chopped walnuts

Combine oil, sugar, eggs and beat well. Sift together flour, salt, soda and cinnamon. Add to creamed mixture. Add vanilla. Fold in pears and nuts. Grease and flour a 10-inch Bundt or tube pan. Spoon in batter. Bake at 325 degrees for 1 hour and 20 minutes, or until cake is done. Let cool in pan for 20 minutes, then remove to cake rack for complete cooling. Drizzle confectioners frosting over cake top, letting some run down the sides. For variation, try an orange or lemon glaze.

Orange Glaze

Blend 2 to 3 tablespoons orange juice and 1 cup sifted powdered sugar to make glaze.

FRENCH PEAR CAKE

1 2/3 cups flour
1 cup sugar
 1/2 teaspoon grated lemon peel
1 teaspoon baking powder
1/2 cup butter, softened
1 egg, beaten
7 or 8 winter pears
1 teaspoon cinnamon
1/8 teaspoon nutmeg
1/8 teaspoon salt
Whipped cream or topping

Combine flour, sugar, lemon peel and baking powder. Cut in butter until crumbly. Set aside 1 1/2 cups of the flour mixture; stir egg into remaining mixture. Press into bottom and about 1 1/2 inches up sides of an ungreased 9-inch spring form pan. Pare, core and slice pears to equal 7 cups; toss with spices. Turn into prepared pan; distribute remaining flour mixture evenly over pears. Bake at 350 degrees about 1 hour or until pears are tender. Cool; remove sides of pan. Cut into wedges and serve with whipped cream. Makes 8 to 10 servings.

FRESH PEAR SHERRY CAKE

1 cup sugar
1/2 cup butter, softened
2 large eggs
2 cups flour
Dash salt
2 teaspoons baking soda
2 teaspoons cinnamon
1/2 teaspoon nutmeg
4 cups fresh pears, peeled, cored and diced
1 cup chopped walnuts
2 teaspoons vanilla
1/4 cup sherry

Beat sugar and butter together until light and fluffy. Add eggs, one at a time, beating well after each. Sift dry ingredients together and mix with creamed mixture. Fold in remaining ingredients. Turn into buttered and floured 9 x 13 inch baking dish. Bake at 350 degrees 35 to 45 minutes. Cool, then frost.

Frosting

Whip 1 cup softened butter until creamy. Add 2 cups powdered sugar and beat again until light and fluffy. Add 1/4 cup sherry, beating well. Frost cooled cake.

PEAR PUDDING CAKE

1 (16 ounce) can pear halves
1 package pound cake mix
1 teaspoon grated lemon peel
2 eggs
1/3 cup chopped walnuts

Drain pears, reserving 3/4 cup syrup. Arrange pears in bottom of greased Bundt pan. Combine the cake mix, lemon peel, eggs, pear syrup and chopped walnuts. Pour batter carefully over pears and bake at 325 degrees for about 1 hour and 15 minutes, until cake tests done. Turn out onto serving plate. Serve with warm sauce.

Lemon Sauce

1 cup sugar
1/2 cup butter
1/4 cup water
1 well-beaten egg
3/4 teaspoon grated lemon peel
3 tablespoons lemon juice
Combine in saucepan and heat gently until boiling. Serve warm over cake.

PEAR UPSIDE-DOWN CAKE

2 tablespoons butter
1/4 cup packed brown sugar
1 can (29 ounce.) pear halves, drained
1 tablespoon red cinnamon candies
1 small jar maraschino cherries
½ cup of walnut halves

Heat oven to 350 degrees. Heat butter in square pan 8 x 8 x 2 inches, or round 9 x 1 1/2 inches, in oven until melted. Sprinkle sugar and candies over butter. Arrange pears on sugar mixture. Decorate with maraschino cherries and walnut halves. Prepare cake as directed. Pour batter over pears. Bake until wooden pick inserted in center comes out clean, 35 to 40 minutes. Immediately invert pan onto heatproof plate; leave pan a few minutes. Remove pan carefully and serve.

Cake

1 1/2 cups biscuit baking mix
1/2 cup sugar
1 egg
1/2 cup milk or reserved pear syrup
2 tablespoons shortening
1 teaspoon vanilla

Beat all ingredients in large bowl on low speed until blended, scraping sides of bowl. Beat on medium speed for 4 minutes. Pour batter over pears and bake.

SPICY PEAR FIESTA

Pear Topping

1/4 cup butter
2/3 cup firmly packed brown sugar
1 tablespoon flour
1 tablespoon pear syrup
1 can (1 pound) pear halves, drained

Melt butter in a 9-inch round layer pan or 9-inch square pan in oven. Stir in brown sugar, flour and pear juice. Place pear halves cut-side down in brown sugar mixture, tips pointing toward the center. Do not place pear in center.

Spice Cake

1 1/2 cups flour
3/4 cup firmly packed brown sugar
1/4 cup sugar
2 teaspoons baking powder
1 teaspoon cinnamon
1/2 teaspoon salt
1/4 teaspoon ground cloves
2/3 cup milk
1/3 cup shortening
1 egg

In large mixer bowl, combine all ingredients at lowest speed until well blended. Pour cake batter over pears, spreading to cover evenly. Bake at 350 degrees for 45 to 50 minutes until top springs back when touched lightly in center. Cool for 2 minutes; invert cake onto serving plate. Serve warm. *For flaming dessert, soak sugar cubes in lemon extract. Place cube in each pear; ignite. Makes 8 servings.

CARAMEL PEAR DROPS

1 (16 ounce) can pears
1/2 cup shortening
1 1/3 cups brown sugar
1 egg
1 3/4 cups sifted flour
1 teaspoon baking soda
1/2 teaspoon salt
1 teaspoon cinnamon
1 teaspoon ground cloves
1/2 teaspoon nutmeg
1 cup chopped walnuts

Drain and dice pears, reserving 2 tablespoons syrup. Cream shortening, sugar and egg until light and fluffy. Sift the dry ingredients and add to creamed mixture. When well blended, stir in reserved 2 tablespoons pear syrup, diced pears and walnuts. Drop by teaspoonfuls onto greased baking sheet. Bake at 350 degrees for 12 to15 minutes. Remove from pan and cool on racks. Spread with caramel icing. Makes 3

Caramel Icing

1/4 cup butter
1/4 cup brown sugar, packed
1 1/2 cups sifted powdered sugar
1/4 teaspoon salt
2 tablespoons light cream

Cook butter and brown sugar until sugar dissolves, about 3 minutes. Add remaining ingredients. Beat till smooth. Spread on cooled cookies.

PEAR OATMEAL COOKIES

1 to 2 fresh pears (1 1/2 cups diced)
I cup sifted flour
1/2 cup butter
1 teaspoon baking powder
1/3 cup honey
1/2 teaspoon salt
1/2 cup brown sugar
1 cup uncooked oatmeal
1 egg
1/3 cup raisins
1 teaspoon vanilla
1/3 cup chopped walnuts

Core and dice unpeeled pears. Measure 1 1/2 cups. Cream butter, brown sugar, and honey. Add egg, beat until fluffy. Add vanilla. Sift together flour, baking powder and salt. Add to creamed mixture. Stir in oatmeal, pears, raisins and nuts. Drop by teaspoonful's on lightly greased baking sheet. Bake at 400 degrees for 10 to 12 minutes. Makes 2 to 3 dozen cookies.

PEAR NUT COOKIES

1 cup flour
1 cup walnuts
1 cup sugar
1/2 teaspoon vanilla
1/2 cup brown sugar
1/2 teaspoon nutmeg
1 cup cooked sliced pears
1/2 teaspoon cinnamon
1 cup butter
1/2 teaspoon baking soda
1 cup almonds

Place all ingredients in food processor. Process until well blended, about 2 minutes. Drop by spoonfuls onto ungreased cookie sheet. Bake at 325 degrees for about 12 minutes. While warm, sift confectioners' sugar over the cookies.

PEAR-DATE FOLDOVERS

1 (16 ounces) can pears, drained and diced
1 cup chopped dates
2 tablespoons sugar
1 teaspoon grated lemon peel
1 cup shortening
1/2 cup granulated sugar
1/2 cup brown sugar 1 egg
3 tablespoons milk 1 teaspoon vanilla
3 cups flour
1/2 teaspoon salt
1/2 teaspoon baking soda

Drain and dice pears, reserving 1/4 cup syrup. Combine diced pears, reserved pear syrup, dates, sugar and lemon peel in small saucepan. Cook over medium heat for 10 minutes. Let cool. Cream shortening and sugars. Add egg milk and vanilla and beat well. Sift together flour, salt and soda. Add to creamed mixture. Mix thoroughly. Chill at least 1 hour. Roll dough and cut into 3-inch circles with cutter. Place about 1 teaspoon of pear- date mixture on each round. Fold over and seal edges with tines of fork. Prick tops. Bake at 350 degrees for 10 to 12 minutes. Makes 3 dozen cookies.

NUTTY BARTLETT BROWNIES

2 eggs
1 cup sugar
2/3 cup butter, melted 1 teaspoon vanilla
3/4 cup flour
1/3 cup unsweetened baking cocoa
1 teaspoon baking powder
1/2 teaspoon salt
1 1/2 cups chopped fresh pears (2 medium pears)
1/2 cup chopped walnuts

Beat the eggs in mixing bowl. Blend in the sugar, melted butter and vanilla. Beat until sugar is dissolved. Combine the flour, cocoa, baking powder and salt. Stir into egg mixture until smooth. Fold in the pears and walnuts. Pour into a greased 8-inch square baking pan. Bake at 350 degrees for 30 to 35 minutes. Cool and cut into squares. Makes 16 small brownies.

PEAR BUTTERSCOTCH BARS

1 (16 ounce) can pears
2 cups all-purpose flour
2 teaspoons baking soda
1 cup light brown sugar
1 teaspoon salt
2 eggs
1/4 cup soft butter
1 (6 ounce) package butterscotch pieces
1/2 cup chopped pecans

Drain and dice pears, reserving syrup. In a large mixing bowl combine pears and reserved syrup with all ingredients except the butterscotch pieces and pecans. Mix until blended at lowest speed of mixer, then beat for 2 minutes at medium speed. Pour batter into greased 9 x 13 inch baking pan. Sprinkle with butterscotch pieces and pecans. Bake at 350 degrees for 35 to 40 minutes. Cool and cut into bars. Makes about 2 dozen bars.

CARAMEL-GLAZED PEAR BARS

1 can (16 ounces) pears
1 cup butter
1 cup granulated sugar
1 cup brown sugar
2 eggs
1 teaspoon vanilla
4 1/2 cups flour
2 teaspoons baking powder
1 teaspoon baking soda
1/2 teaspoon salt
2 teaspoons cinnamon
1 cup raisins
1 cup chopped walnuts
Caramel glaze

Drain pears, reserving syrup. Finely dice pears. Cream butter and sugars until light. Beat in eggs and vanilla.

Sift together flour, baking powder, soda, salt and cinnamon. Add to creamed mixture alternately with 1/2 cup reserved pear syrup. Stir in pears, raisins and nuts. Turn into greased 15 x 10 inch baking pan. Bake at 400 degrees for 15 to 20 minutes. While warm, spread with glaze. Cut into bars. Makes 40 small bars.

Caramel Glaze

In saucepan, combine 1/4 cup brown sugar, 1 tablespoon butter and 2 tablespoons reserved pear syrup. Heat until bubbly. Stir in 1/2 cup powdered sugar. Spread over bars.

PEAR COOKIE SQUARES

3/4 cup butter
3/4 cup brown sugar
2 eggs
1 teaspoon vanilla
3/4 cup wheat germ
1 cup fresh pears, finely chopped (1 or 2 pears)
1 1/2 cups flour
2 teaspoons ginger
1 teaspoon baking soda
1 1/2 teaspoon cinnamon
1/2 teaspoon salt
1/2 cup walnuts, chopped
Orange glaze

Cream butter with sugar. Beat in eggs, vanilla, wheat germ and pears. Combine flour, cinnamon, ginger, baking soda and salt. Mix into creamed mixture. Stir in walnuts. Spread mixture into well-greased 15 x 10 inch baking pan. Bake in 375-degree oven for 20 minutes. While still warm frost with Orange Glaze. Cool completely before cutting into small squares. Makes 3 dozen squares.

Orange Glaze

Mix 1 1/2 cups powdered sugar with 2 tablespoons orange juice and 1 1/2 teaspoon grated orange peel.

BARTLETT BARS

Pear filling

Mix 3 cups chopped fresh pears (2 to 3), 2 tablespoons sugar and 1 cup water in medium saucepan. Bring to boil over medium-high heat. Boil, stirring constantly, for 10 minutes, until mixture thickens. Remove from heat and cool.

Bars

1/2 cup butter, softened
1/4 cup shortening
1 cup brown sugar, packed
1 3/4 cups flour
1/2 teaspoon salt
1/2 teaspoon baking soda
1 1/2 quick cooking oats
1/4 cup finely chopped walnuts

Cream butter with shortening and sugar in large mixing bowl until smooth. Mix flour, salt, soda and oats. Measure 2 cups of crumb mixture and set aside for topping. Add walnuts to remaining crumb mixture and press evenly in bottom of greased 13 x 9 x 2 inch pan. Bake in 400-degree oven 10 to 15 minutes, until golden brown. Remove from oven; cool 10 minutes. Spread pear filling over evenly. Top with reserved crumb mixture, pressing lightly. Bake an additional 25 minutes. While warm cut into bars.

PEAR DATE NUT BARS

4 green pears
1 cup water
1/2 cup walnuts
1/2 cup almonds
1 cup flour
1 cup granulated sugar
1 cup butter
1/2 cup brown sugar
1 teaspoon baking soda
1 teaspoon vanilla
1/2 teaspoon cinnamon
1/2 teaspoon nutmeg
1/2 teaspoon salt
1 egg
1/2 cup raisins
1/2 cup dates
Blanched almonds

Peel, core and slice pears. Cook with 1 cup water for 5 minutes. Toast walnuts and almonds in 375-degree oven for 5 to 8 minutes. In Cuisinart with the metal blade, add flour, sugar, butter, brown sugar, toasted nuts, baking soda, vanilla, cinnamon, nutmeg and salt. Process until blended, about 30 seconds. Add egg, drained cooked pears, dates and raisins. Process until well blended, about 1 minute. Pour into 9 x 12 inch buttered Pyrex baking dish and top with blanched almonds. Bake at 350 degrees for 40 minutes. Cool and cut into bars.

BUTTERSCOTCH PEAR LAYER BARS

Filling

1 (16 ounce) can pears
2 tablespoons cornstarch
1 (6 ounce) package butterscotch chips

Drain pears. Dice and drain again. Combine pears with cornstarch and butterscotch chips and cook over low heat until chips are melted and mixture thickens slightly. Set aside to cool.

Dough

3/4 cup butter
1 cup brown sugar
1 3/4 cups sifted flour
1/2 teaspoon baking soda
1/2 teaspoon salt
1 1/2 cups quick-cooking rolled oats

Cream butter and brown sugar until fluffy. Sift flour, baking soda and salt together. Stir into creamed mixture. Add rolled oats and mix thoroughly. Divide dough in half and pat one part firmly into buttered 9 inch square pan. Spread prepared filling evenly over dough.

Sprinkle with remaining oat mixture. Bake at 400 degrees for 25 minutes. Cool and cut into bars.

PEAR BAR COOKIES

1 1/2 cups sifted flour
1/3 cup granulated sugar
1/3 cup butter
1 large or 2 medium pears
2 large eggs
1/2 cup brown sugar
1/3 cup sifted flour
1/4 teaspoon baking powder
1/4 teaspoon salt
1/4 teaspoon ginger
1/2 teaspoon vanilla
1/2 cup coconut

Combine 1 1/2 cups flour and the granulated sugar; mix well. Cut in butter until particles are fine. Press mixture firmly over bottom of greased 9-inch square pan. Bake at 350 degrees for 20 minutes until edges are lightly browned. Meanwhile, pare, core and dice pear to measure 1 1/4 cups. Beat eggs with brown sugar until light. Stir 1/3 cup flour, baking powder, salt and ginger together. Stir into egg mixture along with vanilla. Fold in diced pear and coconut. Spoon over hot baked layer; spread evenly. Return to oven and bake another 25 minutes until lightly browned. Allow to cool in pan. Cut into bars. Makes 3 dozen bars.

PEAR FAIR SUNDAES

Canned pear halves
Vanilla ice cream
Chocolate, butterscotch or strawberry topping
Whipped cream
Finely chopped walnuts
Maraschino cherry

Take 1 pear half and place in dessert dish. Add 1 or 2 scoops ice cream. Top with your choice of toppings.

Top with whipped cream, sprinkle of chopped walnuts and a maraschino cherry.

KONA PEAR SUNDAES

1/2 cup sugar
2 tablespoons cornstarch
1 1/2 teaspoon dry instant coffee
1 cup water
1 cup chopped winter pears
2 tablespoons butter
2 teaspoons vanilla 1/2 cup pecan halves
3 winter pears, cored and sliced in eighths
6 large scoops chocolate or vanilla ice cream

Combine sugar, cornstarch, and coffee. Gradually stir in water. Add chopped pears; cook and stir over medium heat until sauce thickens and boils. Remove from heat; stir in butter, vanilla and pecans, stirring until butter melts. For each sundae, arrange 4 pear slices in each dish, top with 1 scoop ice cream and spoon about 1/3 cup of pear sauce over ice cream. Serves 6.

SPICED PEAR ICE CREAM

4 medium size ripe pears
1 cup half-and-half
1 cup whipping cream
2/3 cup brown sugar packed
1 teaspoon grated lemon peel
1 tablespoon lemon juice
3/4 teaspoon mace
1/2 teaspoon cinnamon
1/2 teaspoon ground ginger
1/4 teaspoon salt

Halve, core and peel pears. Dice into blender jar and blend to a smooth puree to measure 2 2/3 cups. Combine with all remaining ingredients and stir until well mixed. Freeze in hand-turned or electric ice cream freezer, using 8 parts crushed ice to 1 part rock salt. Freeze until it becomes difficult to turn. Remove dasher. Pour off water from freezer tub and repack, using 4 parts ice to 1 part rock salt. Makes 1 1/2 quarts.

CREAMY MANDARIN PEARS

1/2 pint vanilla ice cream
few drops to 1/4 teaspoon rum flavoring
1 11-ounce can chilled, drained mandarin oranges 4 chilled pear halves, fresh or canned

Stir ice cream to soften; mix flavoring to taste. Arrange mandarin oranges over pear halves in dessert dishes. Spoon softened ice cream over top. Serves 4

FROSTED PEAR SQUARES

8 ounces cream cheese

1 cup sour cream

1 (6 ounce) frozen limeade

4 tablespoons sugar

2 drops green food coloring

1 cup whipping cream, whipped

4 cups diced pears 1 cup coconut

Blend sour cream, frozen limeade, sugar, food coloring and cream cheese. Fold in whipped cream, pears and coconut. Freeze in 9 x 13 inch pan. Take out of the freezer a little while before serving. Serves 8

PEAR-STRAWBERRY SHERBET

3 fresh pears, quartered, cored

1 1/2 cups buttermilk

1/2 cup sugar

2 tablespoons lemon juice

1 teaspoon vanilla

1 pint fresh strawberries

1 egg white

Combine 2 pears with buttermilk, sugar, lemon juice and vanilla in blender. Whirl thoroughly until smooth. Pour mixture into 9-inch pan and freeze until slushy. Finely chop remaining pear and strawberries. Whip egg white until stiff. Fold into frozen mixture along with pear and berries. Freeze until firm. Makes 1 quart.

PEAR SHERBET

2 large ripe pears
1/3 to 1/2 cup low-fat milk
3 packets sugar substitute (optional)

Halve and core pears. Dice unpaired pear halves and spread in a single layer. Quick-freeze, uncovered in the coldest part of the freezer. Put the frozen cubes in a blender or food processor fitted with steel blade. Add the milk and sweetener a little at a time; process quickly, just until mixture resembles soft-serve frozen custard. Serve right away. Makes 4 servings, 70 calories per serving.

PEAR FROZEN YOGURT

Follow above recipe. Substitute 1/2 cup plain low-fat yogurt for milk.

PEAR ICE

1 cup water
1/2 cup sugar
3 to 5 fresh pears
2 tablespoons lemon juice

Bring water and sugar to boil, stirring to dissolve sugar, and boil over medium heat exactly 5 minutes. Cool to room temperature. Core and peel pears; puree in blender or pass through a sieve. Combine pear puree, lemon juice and cooled sugar syrup. Freeze in ice tray until firm, 3 to 4 hours, stirring every 30 minutes. Makes 4 to 6 servings.

BAKED PEARS

Wash, halve and core pears. Put into deep dish, sprinkle with brown sugar or molasses. Dot with butter. Add small amount of water to prevent burning. Cover and bake for 30 minutes at 350 degrees. For variation, stuff centers with honey and almonds, butter and mincemeat, or sprinkle with ginger and lemon juice.

Serve with spice cake, or top with ice cream, orange sherbet, whipped cream or sour cream. Try drizzling a teaspoon of brandy over each pear. Baked pears are delicious both warm and cold.

BAKED GINGERSNAP PEARS

4 medium Bartlett pears
1/4 cup orange juice
1 cup finely crushed gingersnaps
1/4 cup sugar
1/4 cup chopped walnuts
4 tablespoons melted butter

Peel pears, halve and core. Place cut side up in baking dish and drizzle with orange juice. Combine gingersnaps, sugar, nuts and butter. Sprinkle over pears.

Bake at 350 degrees for 20 to 25 minutes. Serve with scoops of vanilla ice cream.

AMBROSIA BAKED PEARS

1 (29 ounce) can pear halves, drained
Orange slices, halved
1/2 cup pear syrup
1/2 cup orange juice
3 tablespoons brown sugar
2 tablespoons cornstarch
1 tablespoon shredded lemon peel
1/4 cup flaked coconut

Drain pears, reserving 1/2 cup syrup. Alternate pear halves and halved
orange slices in baking dish. Combine pear syrup, orange juice, brown
sugar, cornstarch, and lemon peel in saucepan. Cook, stirring until
slightly thickened. Pour over pears and oranges. Sprinkle coconut over
top and bake at 425 degrees for 15 minutes. Serve warm for breakfast,
or chill and serve for dessert. Makes 4 to 6 servings.

GINGER-BAKED PEARS AND APRICOTS

1 1-pound 14-ounce. can pear halves
1 1-pound 14-ounce can whole apricots
2 tablespoons slivered crystallized ginger
4 lemon slices, halved

About 1 hour before serving; heat oven to 325 degrees.
Drain pears, reserving 3/4 cup juice; arrange pears in
2 quart round casserole. Drain apricots, arrange in center of nest of
pears. Sprinkle slivered crystallized ginger over pears and apricots. Tuck
in lemon slices. Pour juice from pears over all. Bake uncovered, 30
minutes. Serve cool. Makes 6 servings.

BAKED PEAR HALVES

Pear Halves:
Place canned pears in shallow baking dish. (12 pear halves)

Fluffy Mixture:
1/4 cup butter
1/2 cup brown sugar
1/4 cup sifted flour
1/2 teaspoon ground ginger

Cream butter, brown sugar, flour and ginger together, beating until fluffy.

Combine:

2 teaspoons lemon juice
1 teaspoon grated lemon rind
1/2 cup liquid from canned pears

Pour over pears. Put equal portions of fluffy mixture on each pear half and bake in 350-degree oven for 30 minutes, until nicely browned. Serves 6

MINT GLAZED PEARS

1 can (1 pound) pear halves, drained
1 (3-ounce) package lime or lemon lime Jell-O
1 cup boiling water
1/2 teaspoon mint extract

Arrange pear halves in skillet. Dissolve Jell-O in boiling water. Add mint extract. Pour over pears. Broil, basting often, until glaze begins to bubble and pears are lightly tinted, about 10 to 12 minutes. Serve warm or chilled. Makes 5 to 8 glazed pear halves.

PEARS WITH RUM CUSTARD SAUCE

3 pears
1/2 cup dates
1/2 cup walnuts
1/4 cup butter
1/4 cup honey
1/2 cup orange juice
nutmeg

Halve and core pears and place in a baking dish. Combine dates and nuts and spoon into centers. Dot with butter and drizzle with honey and orange juice. Sprinkle with nutmeg. Cover and bake at 350 degrees for 30 minutes.

Custard Sauce

1 cup milk
2 egg yolks
2 tablespoons sugar
Salt
1 teaspoon rum extract

Combine remaining ingredients and cook in a saucepan until thick. Pour custard over baked pears. May be served warm or cool.

FLAMBE PEARS

4 fresh pears
1 tablespoon lemon juice
1/4 cup butter
1/4 cup brown sugar, packed
1/4 cup California brandy
Ice cream (optional)

Halve, core, and pare pears. Slice. Sprinkle fruit with lemon juice. Melt butter and add sliced pears. Sprinkle with sugar.

Cook over moderate heat, shaking pan or stirring gently until heated, 3 to 4 minutes. Warm brandy, pour over pears and ignite. Serve plain or spoon over firm coffee or vanilla ice cream. Makes 4 servings.

CINNAMON SPICED PEARS

4 Bosc pears
1/3 cup packed brown sugar
1/3 cup chopped nuts
3 tablespoons melted butter
1/4 teaspoon ground cinnamon
1/4 cup water

Halve and core pears; place cut side up in shallow microwave-proof dish. Combine brown sugar, nuts, butter and cinnamon; spoon into pear halves. Pour water around pears. Microwave uncovered at High 6 minutes or until pears are tender. Turn dish twice during cooking. Makes 8 servings.

Conventional Method:

Place pears in shallow baking dish. Fill and pour water around pears as above. Bake, covered at 350 degrees for 20 minutes or until pears are tender.

Serving tip.   Serve with whipped cream, whipped topping or softened vanilla ice cream.

BARTLETTS WESTERN STYLE

1/4 cup dark seedless raisins
1/4 cup broken walnuts
1/2 cup medium-dry Sherry
2 fresh pears
1/4 cup orange juice
3 tablespoons brown sugar
1/4 cup honey or rum

An hour before serving, mix raisins, walnuts and 1/4 cup Sherry in saucepan. Cover; bring to boil and simmer
3 minutes. Cool. Halve, core and peel pears. Mix juice, sugar and remaining Sherry in pan. Stir over medium heat 15 seconds; add pears and cook 5 minutes, basting constantly. Turn cavities up; fill with raisin-nut mixture. Drizzle with honey or heat 1/4 cup rum, flame and pour over fruit. Makes 4 servings.

SPICED FRESH PEARS

3 cups sugar
1 cup cider vinegar
1 tablespoon coriander seed
3 two-inch pieces stick cinnamon
1-inch piece dried gingerroot
2 pounds firm-ripe pears
Paprika

In a large saucepan, combine sugar, vinegar, coriander seed, cinnamon and gingerroot. Bring mixture to a boil over low heat, and simmer for 5 minutes. Peel, halve and core pears; place a few pieces of pear at a time in the syrup and simmer them for 10 to 15 minutes, or until they are tender. Transfer them to a glass or ceramic bowl; cover and refrigerate. At serving time, give the rounded part of each pear half a blush of paprika. Two pounds of pears should equal 6 to 8 medium pears.

STUFFED PEARS AU CHOCOLAT

6 to 8 fresh pears
1 1/2 cups granulated sugar
2 1/3 cups water
6 lemon slices
3 teaspoons rum flavor
1 package (8 ounce) cream cheese
1/4 cup powdered sugar
2 teaspoons grated lemon rind
2 ounces unsweetened powdered baking chocolate
3 tablespoons butter
Salt

Pare, halve, and core pears. Combine 1 cup sugar, 2 cups water, lemon slices, and 2 teaspoons flavoring in shallow pan. Bring to boil, stirring until sugar dissolves. Add half of the pears; simmer, basting with syrup, turning as needed until fork-tender, about 8 minutes. Remove pears to shallow dish; cook remaining pears in syrup. Chill all pears in syrup several hours. Mix cream cheese with 3 tablespoons syrup from pears and powdered sugar. Beat until smooth and fluffy. Blend in lemon rind and salt. Drain pears. Put halves together with cheese mixture. Chill. Serve with chocolate sauce. To prepare sauce, combine 1/3 cup water with chocolate in saucepan. Cook until blended. Add 1/2 cup sugar and salt. Cook, stirring until sugar dissolves. Remove from heat; stir in butter and rum flavor. Drizzle over pears. Serve warm.

POACHED PEARS WITH GRAND MARNIER CUSTARD SAUCE

2 large lemons
4 to 6 slightly under ripe pears
3 cups cold water
1 cup sugar
1 vanilla bean
Thin strips orange zest (optional)
Grand Marnier Custard Sauce

Squeeze juice from 1 1/2 of the lemons, measure and reserve 3 tablespoons lemon juice. Add remaining juice to large bowl of cold water. Peel pears, being careful not to break off the stem. Using corer or thin-bladed knife core pears from the blossom end, leaving stem intact. Place pears in lemon water. Mix 3 cups water and sugar in saucepan large enough to hold all the pears. Heat stirring frequently, over medium heat until sugar melts and liquid begins to boil. Stir in 3 tablespoons lemon juice. Drain pears and place in simmering syrup. Cook uncovered, turning pears occasionally, over medium heat until tender, about 35 to 45 minutes. Remove from heat. Cut 4 very thin slices from remaining half lemon. Add vanilla bean and lemon slices to poaching liquid. Cool to room temperature. Refrigerate. To serve, remove pears from liquid with slotted spoon. Place on individual dessert plates and spoon custard sauce over each pear. Garnish with orange zest if desired.

GRAND MARNIER CUSTARD SAUCE

6 egg yolks
1/3 cup sugar
1 cup heavy cream
1/2 cup half-and-half
3 to 4 tablespoons Grand Marnier
1/4 teaspoon grated orange zest

Beat egg yolks and sugar with wire whisk in medium saucepan until light in color, about 5 minutes. Scald heavy cream and half-and-half in separate saucepan. Stir hot cream gradually into egg yolks. Cook, stirring constantly, over medium-low heat until sauce thickens and coats a spoon; do not allow to boil. Remove from heat. Stir in Grand Marnier and orange zest. Cool to room temperature. Refrigerate covered until cold.

WINE POACHED PEARS

4 fresh pears
1/2 cup sugar
1/2 cup light corn syrup
1/2 cup sweet sherry or muscatel
1 tablespoon lemon juice
2 tablespoons grated orange peel
1 tablespoon grated lemon peel

Wash, halve, and core pears leaving peels on. Combine sugar, corn syrup, wine, lemon juice and peel in a saucepan. Bring to a boil, stirring until sugar is dissolved. Add pears and simmer gently for about 15 mins. or until pears are tender. Turn pears occasionally during cooking. Put pears in serving dishes. Pour syrup over pears. Serve warm or cold with whipped cream or ice cream.

POACHED PEARS & ORANGE CUSTARD SAUCE

6 fresh pears
1 cup sugar
2 cups water
2 tablespoons lemon juice

Peel pears and core from bottom, leaving stems on. Combine sugar, water and lemon juice and bring to a boil. Place pears in syrup and simmer gently, covered, 10 to 15 minutes or until pears are tender. Baste once or twice during poaching. Remove from syrup and serve warm with Orange Custard Sauce.

Orange Custard Sauce

4 egg yolks
1 cup cream
1/4 cup sugar
Dash salt
1/4 teaspoon grated orange peel
1/4 cup orange juice

Beat egg yolks with sugar and salt. Scald cream with orange peel in top of double boiler. Slowly add to egg yolk mixture. Return to double boiler and cook over hot water, stirring constantly until mixture coats spoon. Stir in orange juice. Serve warm over Poached pears. Makes about 1 1/2 cups custard.

GINGER PEARS

4 cups dry white wine
2 tablespoons sugar
Strip of orange rind, about 2 inches in length
10 paper-thin slices fresh ginger, about 1-inch piece
1 tablespoon vanilla extract
2 teaspoons orange liqueur
1/2 lemon
8 medium size pears

Place wine, sugar, orange rind, ginger, vanilla, and liqueur in a straight sided skillet that will hold the pears snugly. Bring the wine to a boil, reduce heat, cover and simmer the syrup 15 minutes. Meanwhile fill a large mixing bowl with water, and squeeze in the juice of the lemon half. Peel the pears, leaving the stems intact. Remove a slice from the bottom of each pear to ensure that it will stand upright, and drop them into lemon water to keep them from turning brown. Place the pears in the simmering syrup, cover and poach for 15 to 20 minutes. Do not overcook. Remove the pears to a bowl and discard the orange rind and ginger slices. Serve the pears warm, cool, or chilled with the syrup. Serves 8.

PEARS ROMANOFF

6 fresh pears
3/4 cup sugar
3/4 cup water
1 cup whipping cream
6 almond macaroons, crushed
1/2 cup thinly sliced orange

Peel, halve and core the pears. Make a syrup of the sugar and water. Add the pears and simmer until the fruit is tender. Remove the halves of fruit to a serving dish. Add the sliced orange to the syrup and cook until the slices are tender and the syrup is thick. Pour over the pears. Chill. Cover with the whipped cream, sweetened to taste, and sprinkle with the crushed macaroons. Makes 6 servings.

CREAMY PEARS DE MENTHE

3 chilled ripe pears
1 tablespoon lemon juice
1 tablespoon sugar
1 3 ounce package cream cheese
2 tablespoons Cream De Menthe
2 tablespoons confectioners' sugar
1/3 cup heavy cream
Chocolate curls

Halve and core pears. Sprinkle cut surfaces with lemon juice and sugar. Combine cheese, crème de menthe, and powdered sugar. Beat until smooth. Whip cream and blend into cheese mixture. Spoon on to pears. Garnish with chocolate curls. Makes 6 servings.

BARTLETT BERRY BOATS

2 fresh Bartlett pears
Lemon juice
2 tablespoons sugar
1 teaspoon cornstarch
2 tablespoons water
1 cup sliced fresh strawberries
1 tablespoon brandy (optional)

Halve and core pears. Dip cut sides in lemon juice. Combine sugar, cornstarch, water and 1 teaspoon lemon juice in saucepan. Cook, stirring, over low heat until thickened. Add strawberries and brandy. Chill. Spoon glazed strawberries on pear halves. Makes 4 servings. Approx. 90 calories per serving.

PEAR AMBROSIA

2 or 3 fresh pears, chilled
1/2 teaspoon grated orange rind
1/4 cup orange juice
1 tablespoon sugar
1/2 cup flaked coconut

Halve, core and slice pears crosswise into crescents. Combine all ingredients, adding coconut last. Makes 4 or 5 servings.

PEAR COMPOTE

1/4 cup sugar
4 teaspoons cornstarch
3 tablespoons orange juice
1 can whole berry cranberry sauce
Few drops red food color
2 fresh pears
Orange or lemon sherbet

Combine sugar, cornstarch and orange juice in saucepan; stir in cranberry sauce. Cook and stir until mixture is thickened and clear. Stir in red food color. Cool. Halve and core pears. Pare and cut two halves in to cubes. Stir into sauce. Slice remaining halves. Put small scoops of sherbet into 8 stemmed glasses. Ladle cranberry mixture over sherbet; garnish with sliced pears. Makes 8 servings, about 165 calories.

SPICY PEAR COMPOTE

1 can (29 ounce) pear halves in light syrup
1 tablespoon sugar
Dash of allspice
1/2 teaspoon grated lemon rind
10 whole cloves
1 tablespoon lemon juice
1/2 cup shredded coconut

Drain pears; pour pear juice into saucepan; add sugar, allspice, lemon rind and cloves. Bring to boil, simmer gently for 5 minutes. Add lemon juice. Remove cloves, pour juice over pears. Chill. Sprinkle coconut over fruit before serving. Serves 4

WINTER FRUIT COMPOTE

3 firm ripe pears
2 unpeeled medium oranges, sliced
3/4 cup brown sugar
1 cup water
3 tablespoons butter
3 medium baking apples
Seedless raisins

Cut a thin slice off bottom of each pear so they'll stand up. Place pears and orange slices in a 3 quart casserole. Combine brown sugar and water; pour over fruit, be sure to cover orange slices. Dot with butter. Bake uncovered in moderate 350-degree oven for 20 minutes. Core apples, pare strip off top of each. Add to casserole. Fill apple centers with raisins. Bake uncovered 35 to 45 minutes basting fruit occasionally. Serve warm. Makes 6 servings.

PEAR AND CHERRY COMPOTE

2 cans (1 pound, 13 ounces each) pears
3 cans (1 pound each) pitted sweet cherries
1 tablespoon vanilla
Blanched almonds

Drain the syrup from both fruits and simmer juices until reduced to about one-third the original volume. Add vanilla. Put half blanched almond in each cherry. Arrange pears around edge of a large shallow bowl, put cherries in middle, pour the syrup over fruit and chill before serving. Serves 12

PEARS WITH RASPBERRY SAUCE I

Canned pears
Frozen raspberries
Whipped cream

Chill canned pears. To serve, drain and arrange 2 halves in individual bowls. Spoon over slightly thawed frozen raspberries. Top with a puff of whipped cream, and sprinkle with freshly ground nutmeg.

PEARS WITH RASPBERRY SAUCE II

1 pint raspberry sherbet
4 large or 8 small canned pear halves, drained

Put drained pear halves in sherbet dishes (1 large or2 small). Stir about 1 cup raspberry sherbet until soft. Put heaping spoonful on top of each pear half. Serve immediately. Serves 4

PEARS UNDER LEMON SAUCE

4 fresh or canned pear halves
1 package lemon instant pudding
1 cup whipped cream
1 tablespoon lemon rind

Arrange pear halves in dessert dish. Prepare pudding according to package instructions. When almost set, gently fold in whipped cream and lemon rind. Spoon over pears. Chill well and serve. Serves 4.

PEAR COCONUT CRISP

6 fresh pears
1 cup brown sugar, divided
1/2 teaspoon cinnamon
1/2 teaspoon nutmeg
1 teaspoon grated orange peel
1/2 cup flour, divided
1/4 cup orange juice
1/4 cup butter
1 cup flaked coconut

Peel, core and slice pears. Toss with 1/2 cup brown sugar, cinnamon, nutmeg, orange peel and 2 tablespoons flour. Place in shallow baking dish. Pour orange juice over pears. Combine remaining brown sugar and flour. Cut in butter. Stir in coconut and sprinkle over pears. Bake, covered at 350 degrees for 40 minutes. Uncover and bake 10 to 20 more minutes, until pears are tender. Serve warm with cream or half-and-half.

PEAR-DATE CRISP

4 fresh pears
1 cup chopped dates
1/4 cup orange juice
3/4 cup flour
1/2 cup butter, melted
1/2 teaspoon grated orange peel
3/4 cup brown sugar

Core and slice pears. Layer pears and dates in greased 1 1/2 quart baking dish. Pour orange juice over fruit. Combine flour, butter, orange peel and sugar to make crumbly mixture. Sprinkle over fruit and bake at 350 degrees for 40 to 45 minutes. Serve with ice cream or whipped cream.

COCONUT-CREAM PEAR CRISP

3 medium fresh pears, peeled, cored and sliced OR 1 can (29 ounce)
pear halves, drained and sliced
1 1/4 cups milk
1 4-serving size package instant coconut cream pudding
3/4 cup all-purpose flour
1/4 cup chopped nuts
2 tablespoons sugar
1/2 teaspoon ground cinnamon
1/4 cup butter
1 beaten egg
1/2 teaspoon vanilla

Arrange pears in an 8-inch round baking dish. In a bowl combine the
milk and half (5 to 6 tablespoons) of the pudding mix. Pour over pears.
Stir together the remaining pudding mix, flour, walnuts, sugar and
cinnamon. Cut in butter till the size of coarse crumbs. Mix egg and
vanilla. Stir into dry mixture until well combined. Crumble mixture over
top of pears. Bake uncovered, in a 350-degree oven for 40 minutes, or
till top is golden. Serve warm with ice cream, if desired. Makes 4 to 6
servings.

PEARS KAHLUA

5 fresh ripe pears (5 cups)
1/2 cup brown sugar, lightly packed, divided
3/4 cup unsalted soda cracker crumbs
1 teaspoon cinnamon
1/4 cup walnuts, chopped
1/4 cup melted butter
3 tablespoons Kahlua

Peel and cut up pears; place in 8-inch round glass cake pan. Sprinkle on 1/4 cup brown sugar. Combine cracker crumbs, cinnamon, nuts and remaining 1/4 cup brown sugar. Add melted butter and toss to mix. Sprinkle over pears. Microwave on High 10 to 12 minutes, or until pears are tender. If no revolving shelf, turn after 5 minutes. Serve warm topped with Kahlua. Makes 6 servings.

MULLED-WINE PEARS

1-pound can pears
3-inch piece lemon peel
1 cup red table wine
3 ounce package cream cheese
1/2 to 1 cup chopped walnuts

Drain the syrup from a 1-pound can pears; add a 3-inch piece of lemon peel. Stir in 1 cup red table wine. Bring the mixture to a boil, reduce the heat and simmer for 5 minutes. Strain over pear halves and refrigerate. At serving time, fill the centers of the pears with small cream cheese balls that have been rolled in chopped walnuts.

PEAR OATMEAL PUDDING

3 cups sliced pears
1 cup sugar
1 tablespoon flour
1/4 teaspoon salt
1/2 teaspoon nutmeg
1/4 teaspoon cinnamon
3/4 cup oatmeal
1/4 teaspoon baking powder
3/4 cup brown sugar, packed
1/4 cup melted butter

Combine pears, sugar, flour, salt, nutmeg and cinnamon. Spoon into buttered baking dish. Combine oatmeal, baking powder, brown sugar and melted butter. Pat over top of pear mixture. Bake at 350 degrees for 35 to 40 mins. Serve warm, topped with whipped cream.

CRUNCHY PEAR PUDDING

6 fresh pears
1 tablespoon lemon juice
1/2 teaspoon pumpkin pie spice
1/2 cup packed brown sugar
3/4 cup quick cooking oats
1/2 cup melted butter
1/4 cup flour
1/4 teaspoon salt

Pare, halve, core and dice pears to make 4 cups. Place in shallow greased baking dish and sprinkle with lemon juice. Combine remaining ingredients and mix well. Spread over pears. Bake in 375-degree oven for 30 to 35 minutes or until pears are fork tender and top is crisp and lightly browned. Serve warm with cream or ice cream. Makes 6 servings.

PEAR PUDDING

1 1/2 cup flour
1 1/2 teaspoon soda
1/2 teaspoon ginger
2 eggs
1/2 teaspoon vanilla
1 1/2 cups sugar
1/2 teaspoon salt
1/4 teaspoon cloves
3/4 cup pear juice
1 can (2 1/2 size can) pears, drained, sliced

Mix flour, soda, ginger, eggs, vanilla, sugar, salt, cloves and pear juice together. Add the sliced pears. Mix. Pour into greased baking pan. Add topping. TOPPING 3 tablespoons butter, 1/2 cup chopped walnuts, 3/4 cup brown sugar. Mix together until crumbly. Sprinkle over top of cake mixture. Bake in 350-degree oven for one hour. Serve with whipped cream, ice cream or whipped topping.

BUTTERSCOTCH PEARS

1 30-ounce can pear halves
1/3 cup packed light brown sugar
1 cup bite-size toasted rice cereal
2 tablespoons butter, melted
1/4 teaspoon salt
1/4 teaspoon nutmeg
half-and-half

About 30 minutes before serving; preheat oven to 425 degrees. Drain pears. In medium bowl, toss sugar, cereal, melted butter, salt and nutmeg until well mixed. In buttered 9-inch pie plate, sprinkle half of cereal mixture. Arrange pear halves in plate; sprinkle with remaining mixture. Bake 10 minutes or until pears are heated through. Serve with half-and-half. Serves 4 to 6.

GINGER PEAR PUDDING

1 package gingerbread mix
2 fresh pears
1 cup raisins
1/2 cup chopped walnuts

Core and dice pears. Prepare gingerbread mix according to package directions. Stir in diced pears, raisins and walnuts. Pour into greased 6-cup ring mold. Bake at 375 degrees for 1 hour. Unmold immediately onto plate. Fill center with sauce.

Sauce

1/2 cup butter
2 cups powdered sugar
1 teaspoon vanilla
1 egg, separated
Cream butter with sugar. Add vanilla and egg yolk. Mix well. Fold in 1 stiffly beaten egg white. Chill.

PEAR SAUCE

When you have pears that get too ripe, this is a good way to use them. Cut up pears as you would for applesauce. Be sure to core pears first. Add very little water and cinnamon to taste. Cook until pears are done and a soft sauce is formed. May be mashed with potato masher for a smoother sauce. Usually no sugar is needed as the pears are very sweet. Cool and serve with a little whipped cream.

CHOCOLATE PEAR MOUSSE

2 large fresh pears
1 envelope unflavored gelatin
6 tablespoons sugar
1/4 teaspoon salt
3 large eggs, separated
1 (1 ounce) square semi-sweet chocolate cut up
1 teaspoon vanilla
1/2 teaspoon chocolate extract
1/8 teaspoon cinnamon
1/2 cup whipping cream
Whipped cream and chocolate curls for garnish

Pare, core and cut pears into blender jar or food processor and process until finely pureed, to measure 1 1/4 cups. Mix gelatin, 2 tablespoons sugar and salt in top of double boiler. Beat egg yolks lightly. Add to gelatin mixture, along with pureed pear. Set over boiling water and cook, stirring constantly, about 5 minutes until slightly thickened. Add cut-up chocolate and stir until chocolate melts. Remove from heat and stir in vanilla, chocolate extract and cinnamon. Cool until mixture thickens slightly. Beat egg whites to soft peaks. Gradually beat in remaining 4 tablespoons sugar, beating to a soft meringue. With same beater, beat cream to soft peaks. Fold meringue and cream into the thickened gelatin mixture. Turn into soufflé dish 5 3/4 inches diameter, 2 3/4 inches deep or into oiled 1 quart mold and chill firm, at least 3 hours. Shortly before serving, decorate with whipped cream and chocolate curls. Makes 6 to 8 servings. (1 quart)

PEAR-TOPPED GINGERBREAD

1 package gingerbread mix
2 fresh Bartlett pears
1/2 cup brown sugar
1 tablespoon milk
3 tablespoons butter
1/2 teaspoon cinnamon
1/4 cup chopped pecans, walnuts, or almonds

Prepare and bake gingerbread as package directs. Core and slice pears. Combine brown sugar, milk, butter and cinnamon. Heat, stirring to blend. Add nuts. Arrange pear slices in rows on top of gingerbread. Sprinkle with sugar-nut mixture. Broil until topping is hot and bubbly. Serve warm.

CARAMEL PEAR COBBLER

1 can (1 pound, 13 ounce) pear halves, drained reserving 1 cup syrup
1/4 cup flour
1/2 teaspoon grated lemon peel
1/4 teaspoon salt
Dash of ginger
1 cup ginger ale
1 tablespoon butter
1 can Pillsbury Refrigerator Quick Caramel Rolls with nuts

Cube pears, place in 2-quart casserole. In saucepan, combine flour, lemon peel, salt, ginger, ginger ale, reserved syrup, and sugar nut mixture from can of caramel rolls. Mix well. Cook over medium heat, stirring occasionally until thick. Stir in butter. Pour over pears. Separate caramel rolls; arrange on top of sauce. Bake at 400 degrees for 25 to 30 minutes. Serve warm.

PEAR COBBLER

1 cup all-purpose flour
2 tablespoons granulated sugar
1 1/2 teaspoon baking powder
5 tablespoons butter
1 beaten egg
1/4 cup milk
1/2 cup packed brown sugar
4 teaspoons cornstarch
1/4 teaspoon ground cinnamon
1 tablespoon lemon juice
4 cups sliced, peeled pears

Sift together flour, granulated sugar, baking powder, and 1/4 teaspoon salt. Cut in 4 tablespoons butter until it resembles coarse crumbs. Mix egg and milk; stir into flour mixture just till moistened. Set aside. In saucepan mix brown sugar, cornstarch and cinnamon. Stir in lemon juice, remaining butter and 1 cup water or pear juice. Add pears. Cook about 5 minutes. Pour into 8 x 1 1/2 round baking dish. Immediately spoon on flour mixture in 6 mounds. Bake at 400 degrees for 25 to 30 minutes. Serves 6.

SPICY PEAR CRUMBLE

1 (29 ounce) can Bartlett pear halves
1 teaspoon grated lemon peel
1/2 cup flour
1/2 cup quick-cooking rolled oats
1/2 cup packed brown sugar
1/4 teaspoon baking powder
1/2 teaspoon ground cinnamon
1/8 teaspoon salt
1/8 teaspoon ground allspice
1/8 teaspoon nutmeg
1/3 cup butter
1/2 cup finely chopped walnuts
Pear Lemon Sauce

Drain pears; reserve 1 cup syrup for sauce. Slice pears; sprinkle with lemon peel. Mix flour, oats, brown sugar, spices, baking powder and salt. Cut in butter until crumbly; stir in nuts. Place half of mixture in lightly greased 1 1/2 quart baking dish, pressing down lightly. Arrange sliced pears over oat mixture and top with remaining oat mixture. Bake at 350 degrees for 30 to 35 minutes. Serve with Pear-Lemon Sauce. Serves 6

Pear Lemon Sauce

Combine 1 cup reserved pear syrup with 1 tablespoon cornstarch and 1/8 teaspoon nutmeg; cook and stir over medium heat for 5 minutes or until slightly thickened. Add 2 tablespoons butter; remove from heat and add 2 tablespoons lemon juice and 2 teaspoons lemon peel. Serve warm. Makes about 1 cup.

GINGER GLAZED PEAR RING

1 1/2 cups diced fresh pears
1/2 cup raisins
1/3 cup chopped walnuts
1/2 teaspoon grated lemon peel
1 envelope dry yeast
1/4 cup warm water
1 egg
2 1/4 cups buttermilk biscuit mix
6 tablespoons sugar
1 tablespoon butter
Ginger glaze

Combine pears, raisins, nuts and lemon peel. Set aside. Dissolve yeast in warm water. Beat in egg, biscuit mix, and 2 tablespoons sugar. Turn out on floured hoard. Knead about 20 times. Roll into 16 x 9 inch rectangle. Spread evenly with butter, pear mix, and remaining 4 tablespoons sugar. Roll up, from long end. Pinch seam to seal. Place roll, seam side down on greased baking sheet. Shape into ring overlapping ends. Make cuts 2/3 way into ring at 1-inch intervals, turning each cut onto its side. Cover, let raise for 1 hour. Bake at 375 degrees for 15 to 20 minutes. Glaze.

Glaze

1/4 cup water, 1/4 cup sugar, 4 teaspoons corn syrup, 1/2 teaspoon powdered ginger. Combine in saucepan, bring to boil, simmer 5 minutes, stirring constantly. Spoon hot over baked ring.

FRESH PEAR ROLL

One prepared pie crust
4 diced pears
1/4 cup sugar
1/2 teaspoon cinnamon
1/2 teaspoon nutmeg
1/4 cup butter
Confectioners icing

Make crust and roll into a rectangle about 8 x 11 ins. Combine pears, sugar and spices and place in the center of the rectangle. Dot with butter. Carefully fold and seal pastry. Pinch together and place on large baking pan. Bake in 400-degree oven for about 45 minutes. While still warm, drizzle with icing.

CONFECTIONERS ICING

1/2 cup powdered sugar
2 1/2 teaspoons milk
1/4 teaspoon vanilla

Mix all together, mixture will be thin. Drizzle over pear roll. A light sprinkle of cinnamon on top of icing may be added, if desired.

PEAR CUSTARD TART

1 1/4 cups flour
2 tablespoons sugar
Pinch of salt
1/2 cup butter
1 egg, lightly beaten
2/3 cup sugar
1 tablespoon cornstarch
1 egg, lightly beaten
3/4 cup sour cream
3/4 cup heavy cream
2 tablespoons lemon juice
1/2 teaspoon vanilla
1/2 cup fine dry bread crumbs
2 lbs. pears, pared, cored, cut in 1/2 inch thick slices (about 4 to 5 large pears)

In medium bowl stir together flour, sugar and salt. With pastry blender, cut in butter until small crumbs form. Stir in 1 egg until dough forms. Press dough into ball and wrap in wax paper. Refrigerate 30 minutes. On floured surface roll out dough to a 13-inch circle. Line an 11 x 1-inch, or 9 1/2 x 1 1/2- inch tart pan with removable bottom with dough. Trim off excess dough. Refrigerate tart 10 minutes. In medium bowl, stir together 2/3 cup sugar and cornstarch. Stir in 1 egg, sour cream, heavy cream, lemon juice and vanilla until smooth; set aside. Sprinkle bread crumbs in bottom of chilled pastry shell. Arrange pear slices on top of crumbs. Pour custard over pears. Bake at 375 degrees 1 to 1 1/4 hours or until filling is set. Cool.

PEAR CUSTARDS

2 fresh ripe pears
4 large eggs
1/2 cup granulated sugar
1 teaspoon vanilla
1/2 teaspoon salt
2 cups half-and-half
2 teaspoons melted butter
2 tablespoons brown sugar, packed

Halve, core and thinly slice pears. Arrange a few pear slices in bottom of 4 or 5 individual baking dishes, about 1 cup capacity. Cover and set remaining slices aside. Beat eggs with sugar, vanilla and salt. Stir in cream. Pour over pears. Set dishes in shallow pan of hot water. Bake at 325 degrees for 20 to 25 minutes, just until custard is soft-set in center. Remove from oven and water. Toss remaining pear slices with melted butter and brown sugar. Carefully arrange on top of custards and place under broiler for a few minutes until sugar begins to melt. Remove and cool. Serves 4 or 5. Custards are good served for Sunday Brunch.

PEAR BLINTZES

1 1/4 cup Bisquick
2 cups milk
3 eggs
1/4 cup butter, melted
1 package (3 ounce) cream cheese
2 cans (1 pound, 4 ounces each) pear halves, drained
Powdered cardamom
Currant jelly
Butter Sauce (below)

Beat Bisquick, milk, eggs, and melted butter together with beater until blended. Lightly grease a small 6 or 7 inch skillet. Heat until a few drops of water sprinkled on it sizzle. Add about 3 tablespoons butter or just enough to thinly coat bottom of skillet (rotate pan to help coat bottom). Cook until small bubbles appear on surface of pancake. Loosen edges of pancake with a spatula; turn over gently and finish baking on other side. Lay cakes on towel or absorbent paper until ready to fill. These may be made a couple hours ahead of serving. Cut each pear lengthwise in 3 pieces. Spread half of each pancake with a thin coating of softened cream cheese; sprinkle lightly with cardamom; lay 2 slices of pears end to end on cheese. Roll up like a jelly roll. Place rolls in lightly buttered pan, seam side down. Reheat in 400-degree oven for 10 minutes. Serve 2 per person. Garnish with slice of pear, dab of jelly and top with butter sauce. Makes 10 servings.

Butter Sauce

Mix 1/2 cup butter, 1 cup sugar and 3/4 cup light cream in saucepan. Cook 5 minutes over low heat. Stir often and DON'T BURN!

PEAR CREPES

1 cup sugar
1/4 cup water
5 pears peeled and thinly sliced
1/2 teaspoon vanilla
2 tablespoons finely chopped crystallized ginger
 8 to 10 warm cooked crepes
Custard Sauce

In skillet, combine sugar and water; cook over moderate heat for 5 minutes or until syrup is thickened. Add pears, vanilla and ginger. Simmer until pears are tender. Fill crepes; fold over. Top with custard sauce. Makes 8 to 10 crepes.

Custard Sauce

1/4 cup sugar
3 tablespoons flour
1 cup milk
1 egg, beaten
1/2 teaspoon vanilla

Combine sugar and flour in saucepan. Stir in milk and cook over low heat, stirring constantly, until thickened. Remove from heat. Stir a little of the mixture into the beaten egg; return egg mixture to pan. Cook over low heat 2 or 3 minutes. Stir in vanilla. Makes 1 1/4 cups custard.

ALL-PURPOSE CREPE BATTER

4 eggs
1/4 teaspoon salt
2 cups flour
1/4 cups milk
1/4 cup melted butter

In medium mixing bowl, combine eggs and salt. Gradually add flour alternately with milk, beating with an electric mixer or whisk until smooth. Beat in melted butter. Refrigerate batter for at least 1 hour. Cook on up-side down crepe griddle or in traditional pan. Makes about 32 to 36 crepes

PIE PLATE PASTRY

2 cups flour
2 teaspoons sugar
1 1/4 teaspoon salt
2/3 cup salad oil
1 tablespoon milk

Into an 8 or 9 inch pie plate, sift together flour, sugar and salt. With fork, whip together oil and milk and pour over flour mixture. Mix with fork until all flour is dampened (will form a ball in center of plate). Reserve about 1/3 of the dough for top crust if desired. Press remaining dough evenly against bottom and sides of pie plate. Crimp edges. Fill with favorite filling. For top crust, crumble reserved dough in small pieces. Sprinkle over filling. Bade as directed in your recipe or bake at 450 degrees   10 to 12 minutes or until golden. Cool on rack.

STANDARD PASTRY CRUST

2 cups sifted flour
3/4 teaspoon salt
1 cup Crisco shortening
4 tablespoons ice water

Combine flour, salt; cut in Crisco with pastry blender until mixture is uniform (should be fairly coarse). Sprinkle with water, a tablespoon at a time; toss lightly with fork. Work into firm ball; roll out half for bottom crust and half for top crust. Ease pastry into pie plate. Stretching causes shrinkage during baking. Trim pastry 1/2 inch from rim of pie plate. Fill pie. Moisten rim of pie and place top crust over all. Trim edges to within 1/2 inch. Fold over. Crimp edge of crust. Bake as directed. Makes 1 9-inch double crust.

GRAHAM CRACKER CRUMB CRUST

One 9-inch pie plate
1/4 cup butter, melted
I 1/2 cups graham cracker crumbs (18 crackers)
1/4 cup sugar

Melt butter. Blend graham cracker crumbs, sugar and melted butter. Distribute crumbs evenly over bottom and sides of pie plate with fork. Press firmly into place. For perfectly shaped crust, press 8-inch pie plate onto crumbs sliding it against sides to pack and smooth. Form rim by pressing side of finger between two pie plate rims. Proceed around pie. Edges of crumb crusts formed this way do not burn as readily. Bake in 375-degree oven for 8 minutes. Cool on rack before filling. Makes 1 9-inch pie crust.

CREAM CHEESE PASTRY

1/2 cup butter
1 (3 ounce) package cream cheese, at room temperature
1 1/4 cups flour
1/4 teaspoon salt

In large mixer bowl, blend butter and cream cheese with electric mixer. Add flour and salt, all at once, and beat on low speed, just until mixture leaves sides of bowl and forms a ball. Turn dough onto well-floured hoard and roll to a 11-inch circle. Roll onto rolling pin or fold in quarters and transfer to pie plate. Ease pastry into pie plate. Stretching causes shrinkage during baking. Trim pastry 1/2 inch from rim of pie plate. Patch pastry with excess pieces, if necessary. Moisten surfaces to be joined and press together. Moisten underside of overhanging pastry. Fold overhanging edge in half and press together. Crimp edge of crust. Pierce sides and bottom of pastry with fork; refrigerate 1 hour. Bake in preheated 450-degree oven 8 minutes or until golden. Crust is now ready to fill with ready-to-eat filling. For a filling that needs to be baked with the crust, fill unbaked crust and bake as directed in recipe. Makes pastry for 1 9-inch pie plate.

GINGERSNAP CRUST

1 1/2 cups crushed gingersnap crumbs
1/3 cup melted butter

Preheat oven to 375 degrees. Prepare crumbs in blender, or place cookies in strong paper bag and roll fine with rolling pin. Measure crumbs into bowl; toss with melted butter until mixed. Set aside 2 tablespoons crumbs for garnish, if desired. With back of spoon, press rest of mixture to bottom and sides of 9-inch pie plate. Bake 8 minutes, remove to wire rack to cool completely. Fill as recipe directs. Top with garnish.

BASIC AMERICAN CRUST

1 cup all-purpose flour
1/2 teaspoon salt
1/3 cup shortening
1 tablespoon butter
2 to 3 tablespoons water

Combine flour and salt in bowl. Cut in shortening and butter until mixture resembles coarse meal. Sprinkle in water 1 tablespoon at a time, until all flour is moistened and dough comes together. Gather dough into a ball: shape into a flattened round on lightly floured board. Roll out dough to fit size of baking dish. Place over filling; make slits for steam vents: flute edges. Lightly beat. 1 egg yolk with 1 tablespoon water; brush over crust. Bake at 400 degrees for 25 to 35 minutes or until crust turns a golden brown. Serves 8

ALMOND BUTTER CRUST

1 cup all-purpose flour
1/3 cup finely ground almonds
1/2 teaspoon salt
6 tablespoons cold butter
1/4 cup ice water

Combine flour, almonds, and salt in a bowl. Cut in butter until mixture has the consistency of coarse meal. Mix in ice water. Turn onto lightly floured board. Knead dough a few seconds until smooth. Wrap in wax paper; chill 30 minutes before rolling. Makes 1 9-inch crust. Bake as recipe directs.

UPPER CRUST PEAR PIE

5 pears, pared, cored and sliced
2 tablespoons lemon juice
2/3 cup brown sugar
2 tablespoons flour
1/8 teaspoon salt
1/2 teaspoon ground cinnamon
1/2 teaspoon ground cloves

Sprinkle sliced pears with lemon juice; place in a 9 or 10 inch deep dish pie plate or any baking dish that holds the pears comfortably. Combine brown sugar, flour salt and spices. Gently toss with pears to coat evenly. Top with Basic American Crust. Bake as directed below.

PEAR PUMPKIN CUSTARD PIE

1 large pear, peeled, cored and sliced
3 eggs
1 can (1 pound.) pumpkin
1/2 cup brown sugar
1/4 cup granulated sugar
1 teaspoon ground cinnamon
1/4 teaspoon ground ginger
Generous pinch each; nutmeg, cloves and allspice 1/2 teaspoon salt
1 cup light cream
Gingersnap crust, unbaked

In a large bowl beat eggs, slightly; beat in remaining ingredients, except pear, until well blended. Pour filling into prepared gingersnap crust or unbaked pie shell. Arrange sliced pears in a spoke fashion on top of the pumpkin custard. Pears will sink slightly into custard. Bake pie at 350 degrees for 50 to 60 minutes or until knife inserted in center comes out clean.

Cool on rack. Serves 6 to 8. If desired, top each slice with a dollop of Ginger Cream.

Ginger cream;

1 cup heavy cream
2 tablespoons powdered sugar
1/2 teaspoon vanilla
2 tablespoons crystallized ginger, finely cut
In a chilled bowl, beat cream, sugar and vanilla until cream holds a soft shape. Fold in ginger. Serve on custard pie.

PEAR PIE

Pastry for one 2-crust, 9-inch pie
6 pears
3/4 cup sugar
3 tablespoons quick-cooking tapioca
2 tablespoons lemon juice
2 tablespoons butter
1 teaspoon grated lemon peel
1/2 teaspoon nutmeg
1/2 teaspoon cinnamon
1/4 teaspoon salt
Milk

Roll out half of pastry and line a 9-inch pie pan. Peel, core and slice pears into large bowl; add remaining ingredients except milk and toss to mix well. Spoon into piecrust. Roll remaining pastry into 10-inch circle. Brush edges with milk. Place top crust on pie, trim, and decorate edge. Bake 50 to 60 minutes in 425-degree oven until pears are tender and crust nicely browned. Serve warm or cold.

Canned pears may be used. Prepare as above but use 2 cans (29 oz. each) drained and sliced, instead of fresh pears. Bake 40 minutes or until crust is golden.

ALMOND PEAR PIE

1/3 cup butter, softened
1/3 cup sugar
1 egg
1 egg yolk
1/2 teaspoon almond extract
1/2 cup blanched almonds, ground
2 tablespoons flour
3 medium sized pears
Lemon juice
Apricot Jam Glaze
Almond Butter Crust

Cream butter and sugar until light and fluffy. Add whole egg and egg yolk, beating after each addition. Stir in almond extract, almonds and flour. Spread almond cream filling in unbaked Almond Butter Crust. Core, peel and halve pears. Rub with lemon juice. Place pear halves, cut side down on top of almond cream filling. Bake pie at 400 degrees 10 to 15 minutes until pastry begins to brown. Turn down heat to 350 degrees and continue to bake for 15 to 20 minutes. Cool, brush with Apricot Jam Glaze. Makes 6 servings.

Apricot Jam Glaze

1 jar (12 oz.) apricot jam
Juice of 1 lemon
2 tablespoons water
In a saucepan bring ingredients to a boil, stir until smooth, and simmer five minutes. Strain, brush on while still hot. Makes 2 cups glaze. Glaze keeps well stored in refrigerator.

PEAR LIME PARFAIT PIE

1 can (29 ounce) canned pear halves
1 package (3 ounce) lime flavored gelatin
1 pint vanilla ice cream
Whipped cream
Prepared graham cracker pie crust

Drain pear halves, reserving 1 cup syrup. Heat syrup to boiling and pour into blender. Add gelatin and blend until dissolved. Add ice cream by spoonful, blending after each. Place container if refrigerator and chill until mixture mounds when dropped from a spoon. Set aside 3 pear halves. Add remaining pear halves to gelatin mixture and whirl until blended. Return to refrigerator to chill. When partially set, spoon into graham cracker pie crust, pile whipped cream in pie center, garnish with slices from the 3 reserved pears. Serves 6 to 8.

GINGERSNAP PEAR PIE

1 (16 ounce) can pear halves
1 envelope unflavored gelatin
1/2 cup sugar, divided
1/2 teaspoon ginger
3 eggs, separated
1 1/4 cups light cream
1 teaspoon vanilla
1/2 cup heavy whipping cream
1 (9-inch) baked gingersnap crumb crust

Drain and slice pears. Combine gelatin with 1/4 cup sugar, salt and ginger. Beat egg yolks slightly. Stir in light cream and gelatin mixture. Cook in double boiler over hot water, stirring constantly until mixture coats spoon, about 15 minutes. Stir in vanilla and cool until mixture mounds slightly when dropped from spoon. Beat just enough to make smooth. Beat egg whites until frothy and gradually add remaining 1/4 cup sugar, beating until stiff peaks form. Whip cream. Fold both into gelatin mixture. Cover bottom of crumb crust with ½ of cream filling. Arrange a layer of pear slices over filling, reserving 6 slices for garnish. Spread remaining filling over pears. Sprinkle top with gingersnap crumbs and arrange remaining pear slices on top. Chill until firm. Serves 8.

FARMHOUSE PEAR PIE

1 package active dry yeast
1/4 cup warm water, about 110 degrees
1/2 cup butter, softened
1 1/2 to 2 cups flour
1/4 teaspoon salt
4 to 5 (about 6 cups) Bosc pears, peeled, cored and sliced
2 tablespoons orange juice
1 teaspoon grated orange peel
1/3 cup sugar
3 tablespoons cornstarch
1 teaspoon cinnamon
Orange glaze

Dissolve yeast in warm water. In a large mixer bowl, combine yeast mixture, butter, 1/2 cup flour and salt; beat 5 minutes. Gradually beat in 1 cup additional flour to make a soft dough. Knead dough on floured board, kneading in additional flour to make a smooth dough. Roll dough in circle 18 inches in diameter; gently lift onto greased baking sheet. Gently toss pears with orange juice and peel. Combine sugar, cornstarch and cinnamon; mix gently with pears. Spoon pear mixture onto dough leaving a 4 to 5-inch border. Lift edges of dough up and over fruit, leaving a 5-inch circle of pears showing in center. Bake at 350 degrees 30 to 35 minutes or until crust is golden brown and pears are tender. Drizzle with Orange Glaze. Makes 10 to 12 servings.

Orange Glaze

Combine 3/4 cup powdered sugar, 1 tablespoon orange juice and 1/4 teaspoon grated orange peel.

PEAR CHEESE PIE

1 (1 pound) can pear halves, well drained
1 9-inch graham cracker crust
2 well-beaten egg yolks
1 8-ounce package cream cheese
1 cup dairy sour cream
1/2 teaspoon grated lemon peel
1 teaspoon lemon juice
1/2 cup sugar
1 tablespoon all-purpose flour
1/2 teaspoon salt
1/2 teaspoon nutmeg
2 egg whites
1/4 teaspoon cream of tartar
1/4 cup sugar

Slice pears into graham cracker crust. Combine egg yolks and softened cream cheese, beat smooth. Blend in sour cream, lemon peel, and lemon juice. Combine 1/2 cup sugar, flour, salt and nutmeg; add to cheese mixture. Mix well. Pour over pears. Bake at 375 degrees for about 25 minutes or till just set. Meanwhile beat egg whites with cream of tartar until frothy. Gradually add 1/4 cup sugar, beating till stiff peaks form. Spread meringue over filling, sealing to edges of crust. Bake another 10 minutes longer or until meringue is golden brown. Makes 8 servings.

NATURAL CHEDDAR PEAR PIE

Unbaked 9-inch pie shell
5 fresh pears
1 tablespoon flour
1/3 cup sugar
 1/2 teaspoon ground ginger
1/8 teaspoon salt

Pare, core and slice pears. Combine sugar, flour, ginger, and salt. Mix with pears and turn into pastry shell. Sprinkle on Cheese Crumble Topping. Bake, below oven center, in 425-degree oven until pears are tender and crust is crisp and golden brown, about 40 to 45 minutes. Makes 1 9-inch pie.

Cheese Crumble Topping

Combine 1/3 cup sifted flour, 1/4 teaspoon salt, 3 tablespoons sugar, 1/3 cup shredded sharp natural Cheddar cheese and 3 tablespoons melted butter.

LEMON PEAR PIE

Prepared gingersnap crust
1 package, 4 ounce lemon pie filling
2 fresh pears
1 tablespoon fresh lemon juice

Bake gingersnap crust as directed. Cool. Prepare lemon pie filling as directed on package, cool slightly. Pare, halve and core pears. Cut into 1/4-inch slices. Stir pears and lemon juice into lemon filling. Turn into prepared crust. Prepare meringue as pie filling package directs. Spread over filling. Bake at 425 degrees for 3 to 5 minutes. Serves 6 to 8.

SOUR CREAM PEAR PIE

Unbaked 9-inch pie shell
5 or 6 pears
1 to 2 teaspoons lemon juice
1/3 cup flour
3/4 cup sugar
1/4 teaspoon salt
1/4 teaspoon ginger
1 teaspoon cinnamon
1/4 cup butter
1/2 cup sour cream

Peel and slice pears. Toss with lemon juice. Pile into the unbaked pie shell. Mix together flour, sugar, salt and spices. Cut in butter. Spoon mixture over pears. Spread sour cream on top of sugar mixture. Bake at 400 degrees for 25 minutes. Reduce heat to 350 degrees, bake for 20 more minutes. Delicious served warm. Serves 8.

PEAR AND RAISIN PIE

Unbaked 9-inch pie shell
1 cup raisins
2 fresh winter pears
2/3 cup honey
1/3 cup half-and-half
2 teaspoons. grated orange
Nutmeg
1/4 cup flour

Line pie plate with pastry. Place raisins in bottom. Pare, core and thinly slice pears. Arrange in circle on top of raisins. Combine honey, half-and-half, and flour. Pour over fruit. Sprinkle with nutmeg. Bake at 425 degrees 40 to 50 minutes, until pears are tender. Makes 1 9-inch pie. Serves 6 to 8

GOLDEN PEAR PIE

Pastry for 2 crust 9-inch pie
Lemon juice
1/2 cup dried apricots
1/4 cup chopped nuts
2 tablespoons flour
4 fresh winter pears
1/4 teaspoon cinnamon
1/2 cup brown sugar
 Dash salt
2 tablespoons butter

Core and slice pears. Sprinkle with lemon juice and set aside. Cover apricots with water. Bring to boil and simmer 10 minutes. Drain and dice. Combine pears, apricots, brown sugar, flour, nuts, cinnamon and salt. Line a 9-inch pie plate with pastry. Fill with pear mixture. Dot with butter. Top with lattice crust and flute edges. Bake at 425 degrees 45 to 50 minutes. Makes 1 9-inch pies. Serves 6 to 8.

PEAR-MINCE PIE

Pastry for 2 crust 9-inch pie
6 cups 1/4-inch peeled pear cubes
1 1/2 cups raisins
1/2 cup currants
3/4 cup packed brown sugar
1 cup chopped candied lemon peel
1 1/2 teaspoons cinnamon
1 1/2 teaspoons nutmeg
1 teaspoon cloves
1/2 teaspoon salt
1 cup apple cider or apple juice

In 3-quart or larger saucepan, combine all ingredients for filling. Stir occasionally over medium heat 1 to 1 1/2 hours until pears are tender and sauce is syrupy. If necessary, add water to prevent mixture from becoming completely dry. Line a 9-inch pie plate with prepared pastry. Spoon filling into unbaked pie shell. Roll out remaining dough to 12-inch circle. Cut slits as desired. Cover pie, trim and flute edge. Cover edge of pie with foil. Bake at 375 degrees for 25 minutes. Remove foil. Bake 25 to 30 minutes longer until crust is golden brown. Cool. Serves 6 to 8

PEAR RHUBARB PIE

1 can (29 ounce) pears cut in 1/2-inch pieces
1 cup sugar
1/3 cup flour
2 1/2 cups fresh rhubarb
1/4 teaspoon mace
1/2 teaspoon salt
Pastry for 2-crust 9-inch pie
2 tablespoons butter

Drain pears. Cut into bite-size chunks and toss with rhubarb. Place half of fruit in pastry-lined pie plate. Combine sugar, flour, salt and mace. Sprinkle half over fruit. Add remaining fruit and top with remaining sugar mixture. Dot with butter. Place woven lattice crust over pie. Seal and flute edges. Sprinkle lightly with sugar. Bake at 450 degrees 10 minutes. Reduce to 350 heat and continue baking 40 minutes. Serve warm as is, or with ice cream. Makes 6 to 8 servings.

BRANDIED BARTLETT PEAR PIE

6 cups green Bartlett pears, Peeled, cored and sliced
1/2 teaspoon cinnamon
3/4 cup sugar
1/2 teaspoon nutmeg
2 tablespoon. brown sugar
3 tablespoons Brandy
3 tablespoons. corn starch
3 tablespoons Amaretto
3 tablespoons unsalted butter
Pastry for 2-crust pie shell

Mix all ingredients, pour into an unbaked pie shell. Cover with top crust. Bake at 400 degrees for 45 minutes. Makes 1 9-inch pie.

GINGER-CRUMB PEAR PIE

1/4 teaspoon ginger
1/4 cup sugar
2 tablespoons flour
5 to 6 sliced fresh pears
Pastry for 9-inch pie shell
4 teaspoons lemon juice
1/2 cup Karo syrup
Crumb Topping

Mix sugar, flour and ginger together as a thickening. Toss lightly with sliced pears. Pile into the pie crust. Sprinkle with lemon juice and syrup. Press crumb top on. Bake at 450 degrees for 15 minutes, reduce heat to 325 degrees and bake for another 20 to 30 minutes. Serves 8

Crumb Topping

1/3 cup butter, 1/3 cup brown sugar, 2/3 cups flour Combine flour, sugar and butter together. Cut or mix with fork till mixture is like coarse crumbs.

PEACH'N PEAR PIE

3 cups sliced peaches
few grains salt
2 cups sliced pears
1 tablespoon butter, cut in bits
3/4 cup sugar
1 tablespoon tapioca
1 tablespoon lemon juice
1 teaspoon sugar
1/8 teaspoon cinnamon
Pastry for 2-crust pie

Mix first 8 ingredients. Line a 9-inch pie pan with pastry. Pour in peach and pear mixture. Cover with top crust. Seal, flute and prick with fork. Brush lightly with cold water. Sprinkle with 1 teaspoon sugar. Bake on lowest rack in oven at 400 degrees for 40 to 50 minutes. Makes 1 9-inch pie.

PEAR CRUMBLE PIE

1 9-inch pie shell
3 tablespoons sugar
3 tablespoons cornstarch
Dash salt
1 teaspoon grated lemon rind
1/2 teaspoon ginger
3 tablespoons lemon juice
1 1/2 to 2 cans (13 oz.) drained pears or 6 to 8 sliced fresh pears
1 cube butter
1 cup flour
1/2 cup brown sugar
1/2 teaspoon cinnamon

Mix sugar, cornstarch, salt, lemon rind and lemon juice and toss with pears. Arrange in pie shell. Mix butter, flour, brown sugar and spices until crumbly. Sprinkle over pears. Bake in 425-degree oven for 30 to 35 minutes (longer if using fresh pears). Makes 1 9-inch pie.

APPLE-PEAR CRUNCH PIE

2 cups sliced pared tart apples (2 or 3 apples)
3 1/2 cups sliced pears, peeled (4 to 5 pears) 1 cup sugar
3 tablespoons flour
1/2 teaspoon cinnamon
1/4 teaspoon salt
1/2 teaspoon grated lemon rind
1 tablespoon lemon juice
Crunch topping
1 9-inch unbaked pie shell

Combine pears and apples. Sprinkle with lemon juice and lemon rind. Combine sugar, flour, cinnamon and salt; sprinkle over fruit. Toss gently, place in pie shell. Top with Crunch topping. Bake at 400 degrees 15 minutes. Cover lightly with foil and continue baking 20 to 30 minutes or until fruit is tender.

Crunch Topping

1/2 cup flour
1/2 cup brown sugar
4 tablespoons butter
1/2 cup chopped walnuts
Combine flour, brown sugar in a bowl. Cut in butter until mixture is crumbly; stir in walnuts. Spoon over pie.

PEAR CRUNCH PIE

Pastry for one-crust 9-inch pie
TOPPING
1 cup sifted flour
1/2 cup packed brown sugar
1/2 cup butter
1/4 teaspoon cinnamon
1/4 teaspoon nutmeg
1/2 cup chopped pecans

Combine flour, sugar, cinnamon and nutmeg. Add butter and cut in till mixture is like coarse crumbs. Stir in chopped pecans. Set aside.

Pie Filling

1 can (29 ounce) pear halves, drained, reserving syrup 1/4 cup sugar
2 tablespoons cornstarch
1/8 teaspoon nutmeg
1 1/2 cups liquid, pear juice plus water if needed 1 tablespoon butter
1 teaspoon grated lemon peel
1 tablespoon lemon juice

Line a 9-inch pie pan with crust. Slice pear halves and arrange in bottom of crust. Combine sugar, cornstarch, nutmeg and liquid in saucepan and cook over medium heat stirring constantly until thickened, about 5 minutes. Add butter, lemon peel and lemon juice. Stir. Pour over pears in pie pan. Top with Crumb topping and bake at 425 degrees for 20 to 25 minutes. May be served warm or cold with whipped cream. Serves 8.

CARAMEL NUT PEAR PIE

6 cups sliced fresh pears
1/2 cup sugar
2 tablespoons tapioca
3/4 teaspoon cinnamon
1/4 teaspoon nutmeg
1 tablespoon lemon juice
1/4 teaspoon salt
1 unbaked 9-inch pastry shell
3/4 cup oatmeal
1/4 cup butter
3 tablespoons sugar
1 tablespoon flour

Core and slice unpeeled pears. Toss with sugar, tapioca, spices, lemon juice and salt. Pile into pastry shell. Combine oatmeal, butter, sugar and flour. Crumble over pears in pastry shell. Bake at 400 degrees for 45 to 50 minutes. Drizzle with Caramel nut mixture.

Caramel Nut Mixture

18 candy caramels
5 tablespoons milk
1/4 cup chopped nuts
Cook over medium heat until melted. Pour over pie.

Bake 8 minutes longer. Cool. Makes 8 servings.

2017 PEAR PEARFECTION ADDITIONS

1890's

PEAR PICKLE

Select small, sound ones, remove the blossom end, stick them with a fork, allow to each quart of pears one pint of cider vinegar and one cup of sugar, put in a teaspoonful allspice, cinnamon and cloves to boil with the vinegar; then add the pears and boil, and seal in jars.

BAKED PEARS

Pare and core the pears, without dividing; place them in a pan, and fill up the orifice with brown sugar; add a little water, and let them bake until perfectly tender. Nice with sweet cream and boiled custard.

PEAR PUDDING

Pare some nice, ripe pears, (to weigh) about three fourth of a pound. Put them in a sauce-pan with a few cloves, some lemon or orange peel and stew about a quarter of an hour in two cupsful of water; put them in your pudding dish, and having made the following custard, one pint of cream or milk, four eggs, sugar to taste, a pinch of salt and a tablespoon of flour; beat eggs and sugar well, add the flour, grate some nutmeg, add the cream by degrees, stirring all the time – pour this over the pears, and bake in a quick oven. Serve cold with sweetened cream.

1920's

BOILED TONGUE WITH PEAR

Clean and trim fresh beef tongue.
25 cent soup bone
10 cent soup vegetables
Two cloves
Small piece bay leaf
Add two small cans of tomato sauce after tongue is boiling, one half apple or pear (fresh, salt and pepper to taste. Remove tongue and skin (saving liquor for soup. Slice thinly and serve with garnish of boiled vegetables.

PEARLETTES

3/4 cup warm, not hot water
1 package active dry yeast
2 1/2 cups prepared biscuit mix
2 tablespoons sugar filling
Melted butter or margarine
1 pear, sliced
3 tablespoons sugar
1 teaspoon cinnamon
1/2 teaspoon ginger

Measure warm, not hot, water into a mixing bowl. Sprinkle in yeast. Stir until dissolved. Add biscuit mix and beat 60 times. Turn on well-floured board and form into smooth ball. Let rest 5 to 10 minutes. Roll dough out to ¼ inch thickness. Cut into rectangles 2 x 4 inches. Brush with butter or margarine. Place pear slices lengthwise, down center third of the rectangles. Combine sugar, cinnamon and ginger and sprinkle over pears. Cut slits in dough along each side of the filling making strips about ½ inch wide. Fold strips at an angle across filling, alternating from side to side. Place on greased baking sheet. Let rise in a warm place, free from draft for about 1 hour. Bake at 350 degrees about 15 to 20 minutes. Makes 15 rolls.

FRENCH FRIED PEARS

Drain canned pears thoroughly. Dip the pear halves in cracker crumbs then in beaten egg diluted with milk (1 tablespoon of milk each egg) serve hot with a main course. and then in cracker crumbs again. Fry in deep hot fat at 375 degrees until a delicate brown. Pineapple, peaches or bananas may be prepared in the same way.

1930'S

PARTY PEAR PUNCH

Combine equal parts pear whole fruit nectar and ginger ale in a star or ring shaped mold to float atop your party punch bowl. Add red maraschino cherries and pieces of canned fruit cocktail to the nectar for extra color.

PEAR DUMPLINGS

1 1/2 cups sifted flour
1 1/2 teaspoons baking powder
2/4 teaspoon salt
1/4 cup shortening
1/2 cup milk
2 pears
4 tablespoons brown sugar, cane or beet
4 teaspoons butter or margarine.

Sift together flour, baking powder and salt. Cut in shortening. Add milk and mix well. Divide dough into four parts and roll each to a circle about 6 or 7 inches in diameter) depending on size of pears. Halve and core pears. Place a pear half on center of each piece of dough. Put 1 tablespoon of brown sugar and 1 teaspoon of butter or margarine on each pear half. Fold edges of dough up over fruit and seal edges together. Place dumplings in a shallow greased pan or on a baking sheet. Bake at 400 degrees about 40 minutes, or until pastry is browned and pears are tender. Serve warm with orange sauce.

1940'S

PEAR AND APRICOT PRESERVES

One cup of dried apricots
4 cups of water
9 cups of prepared pears
5 cups of beet or cane sugar
3/4 teaspoon salt.

Wash the apricots, cut in narrow strips with scissors. Place in a large preserving kettle. Add the water, bring to a boil and simmer, covered, about fifteen minutes. Wash and pare about 4 ½ pounds of the firm, ripe pears. Cut into eights, remove the cores and cut crosswise in thin slices. Weigh or measure. Add to the apricots, bring to a boil and simmer, covered, about fifteen minutes, or until the pears are tender. Add the sugar and the salt and mix well. Cook slowly until the mixture boils, stirring only until the sugar is dissolved. Boil, rapidly about ten minutes or until the fruit is clear and the desired consistency is reached, stirring frequently. Pour into clean, hot, sterilized jars or glasses and seal at once. Makes 7 half pint jars or 10 six ounce glasses.

PEAR HONEY

The recipe for pear honey yields the spread itself, plus a thick rind less marmalade which makes a scrumptious topping for butter cookies

8 cups pears, finely chopped
1/4 cup water
6 cups sugar
Juice of 1 lemon
1 teaspoon powdered ginger
2 tablespoons concentrated frozen orange juice.

Wash, pare, pit and finely chop pears. The pears may be put through a food grinder. The finer they are chopped, the clearer the product. Place in a saucepan. Add water, bring to a boil and allow to boil 10 minutes.

Add sugar, lemon juice, ginger and orange juice. Mix well. Bring mixture to a full boil and boil until thick, about 40 minutes. Strain out pieces of fruit. Pour into jars. Seal at once. Makes 5 jelly jars of clear honey or 2 jars thick pear marmalade.

FRENCH PANCAKES FILLED WITH PEARS

3 pears skinned, cored and cut up roughly
2 tablespoons pear, apricot or peach jam
Grated rind of 1/2 lemon
Grated rind of 1/2 orange
2 tablespoons granulated sugar
1/3 cup water

Cook ingredients slowly until quite soft. Fill crepes, and serve with the following sauce: Put in pan grated rind and juice of one orange and one lemon, three tablespoons apricot, pear or peach jam, two tablespoons granulated sugar and ½ cup water. Simmer until syrupy. A good tablespoon of butter may be stirred into the sauce at the last moment. Blanched pistachio nuts or almonds may also be added. Serves five to six.

French Pancakes (Crepes)

    1 cup all-purpose flour (spooned and leveled)
    1 tablespoon sugar
    1/4 teaspoon coarse salt
    1 1/2 cups whole milk
    4 large eggs
    3 tablespoons unsalted butter, melted

Mix all the dry ingredients. Add milk and eggs together, separately and whisk till blend. Add to the dry mixture and then whisk everything until well blended. Let batter sit at least 15 minutes at room temperature. Heat a 9-inch skillet over medium. Lightly coat with butter. Add 1/4 cup batter and swirl to completely cover bottom of skillet. Cook until underside of crepe is golden brown, 2 to 3 minutes. Loosen edge of crepe with a rubber spatula, then with your fingertips, quickly flip. Cook 1 minute more. Slide crepe out of skillet and repeat with remaining batter. (Coat pan with butter as needed.) Makes 6 to 8 crepes.

1950'S

PARADISE SHAMROCK SALAD

1 number 2 1/2 can Bartlett pears, tinted green
1 pound cottage cheese
Salad greens
Green Pepper
Mayonnaise honey dressing

To tint pears green. Drain juice from can of pears. Add green food coloring as desired to tint pears a bright color. It takes about ¼ teaspoon of coloring. Allow pear halves to remain submerged in tinted juice until desired amount of color is absorbed. Remove pear halves from juice and drain. Tinted juice may be added to other fruit juices to make emerald punch.

Assemble: On each of three salad plates, arrange bed of greens. In center, place mound of cottage cheese. On cheese, arrange three green pear halves to resemble shamrock, using strip of green pepper to resemble stem. Garnish with mayonnaise-honey dressing.

Mayonnaise Honey Dressing

1/4 cup mayonnaise
1 tablespoon prepared mustard
1 tablespoon honey
1/2 tablespoon lemon juice

In a small bowl, whisk together the mayonnaise, mustard, honey and lemon juice. Store covered in the refrigerator

PEAR CRUNCH PIE

Line a 9 inch pie pan with pastry.
Blend: 1 cup flour, 1/2 cup margarine, 1/2 cup brown sugar,
cinnamon and nutmeg. Crumble until in coarse crumbs.
Drain a 2 1/2 can of pear halves, reserving syrup.
Combine: 1/4 cup sugar, 2 tablespoons cornstarch, 1/8 teaspoon salt,
1/2 teaspoon nutmeg
1 1/2 cups liquid (pear juice and lemon juice)
Put in a 2 quart sauce pan and cook for five minutes or until clear.
Add: 1 tablespoon butter, 1 tablespoon lemon rind.
Arrange the pears cut in eights. Top with crumb mixture and sprinkle
with chopped pecans. Bake at 425 degrees 20 to 25 minutes.

PEAR DELICIOUS

1/2 cup butter
12 canned pears
2 teaspoons lemon juice
1 teaspoon grated lemon rind
1/2 cup pear liquid
1/2 cup brown sugar
1/4 cup sifted flour
1/2 teaspoon ground ginger.

Place pears, cut side up in shallow pan. Combine lemon juice, lemon
rind and pear liquid and pour around pears. Cream butter, add sugar,
flour and ginger. Beat until light and fluffy. Place equal portions on
each pear half. Bake at 350 degrees for 30 minutes or until brown and
crusty. Serve warm. Serves 6.

BAKED PEARS

2 cans No. 2 pears
1/2 cup brown sugar
1/2 cup cube butter sliced
Cinnamon or allspice to taste.

Place pears in Pyrex utility dish and pour juice over pears. Sprinkle brown sugar and spice over pears and dot each one with butter. Place in oven and bake for about I hour, basting frequently. Serve with cream or ice-cream. Fresh pears may be used in this recipe.

BANANA NUT BREAD

1 3/4 cups sifted all-purpose flour
2 teaspoons baking powder
1/4 teaspoon baking soda
1/2 teaspoon salt
1/3 cup soft shortening
2/3 cup granulated sugar
2 eggs unbeaten
1/2 cup mashed ripe bananas
1/2 cup nuts

Start heating oven to 350 degrees and grease 9x5x3 inch loaf pan. Sift flour, baking powder, soda and salt. With electric mixer at medium speed, thoroughly mix shortening with sugar and then with eggs until light and fluffy (about 4 minutes. Then at low speed beat in flour mixture alternately with bananas until smooth. Then add nuts and turn into pan. Bake one hour. Cool 10 minutes and remove from pan. Leave overnight before slicing.

PEAR PINEAPPLE CHEESE PIE

1/2 cup pear syrup
1/4 cup pineapple syrup
1/4 cup cornstarch
1/4 cup sugar
1/8 teaspoon salt
Dash of nutmeg
1/4 teaspoon vanilla
1 tablespoon butter
1 1/2 cups shredded Cheddar Cheese
1 pie pastry lining a 9 inch pie plate
6 canned pear halves
2 1/2 cups pineapple chunks
egg white

Sour Cream Topping
2 cups Dairy sour cream
2 tablespoons combined pear and pineapple syrup
2 tablespoons confectioners' sugar

Mix small amount of combine pear and pineapple syrups with
cornstarch to blend; then add remaining syrups. Cook until clear and
thickened. Remove from heat, stir in sugar, salt, nutmeg, vanilla, butter
and cheddar cheese. Line pie plate with pastry. Arrange pears, cut side
up with narrow ends toward center. Arrange pineapple chunks arounds
pear. Spread sauce over fruit. Cut remaining pastry into strips and make
a latticed top. Bakes 12 minutes. Lower heat to 375 degrees and bake
35 more minutes. Serve with sour cream topping. (brush top with egg
white to give golden glaze.

1960s and 1970's

ENGLISH PEAR PIE

2 cups dried Bartlett pears
1/2 cup sugar.
1/8 teaspoon salt
1/2 teaspoon cloves
1 nine inch pie crust

Wash dried pears. Soak overnight in water enough to cover; drain, remove cores, and put in earthenware or glass pie plate. Mix sugar, salt and cloves and sprinkle over the pears. Moisten the edges of the baking dish and put a layer of pastry over the top. Bake 30 minutes, putting into a hot oven and after 10 minutes reducing the heat; cool slightly, turn upside down on a plate and serve immediately. Heap whipped cream or ice cream on each serving if desired.

1-2-3-4 PEAR CAKE

1 can (1 poune) pear halves or pieces
1 package Balter cake mix (or cake mix of your choice)
3 eggs

Combine pears and syrup, cake mix and eggs in large mixing bowl. Blend at low speed until all ingredients are moistened. Beat 4 minutes at medium speed. Pour into greased 9 x 13 inch cake pan or fill cupcake liners 2/3 full. Bake at 350 degrees for 30-40 minutes for sheet cake, 25-30 minutes for cupcakes. Frost while warm with the following:

Lemon Glaze (frosting)

1 cup sifted powder sugar
1 lemon (juice and grated peel)

Beat powdered sugar with lemon juice and grated peel until smooth. Drizzle over warm cake.

DELTA PEAR CAKE

1 1/2 cups vegetable oil
2 cups sugar
3 eggs
3 cups sifted flour
1 teaspoon salt
1 teaspoon baking soda
1 teaspoon cinnamon
1 teaspoon vanilla
2 cups peeled and chopped pears
1 cup chopped nuts

Combine oil, sugar and eggs; beat well. Sift together flour, salt, baking soda and cinnamon. Add to creamed mixture. Add vanilla. Fold in pears and nuts. Grease and flour a 10-inch Bundt or tube pan. Spoon in batter. Bake at 325 degrees for 1 hour and 20 minutes or until cake is done.

Let cool in pan for 20 minutes and remove to a cake rack for complete cooling. Drizzle confectioners frosting over cake top, letting some run down the sides. For variation, try an orange or lemon glaze. (Frosting is optional.) May use canned pears. Serves 12

PEAR SANDWICH

Halve and core the pears before spreading with cream cheese or peanut butter. Put pears back together if you want a "healthy" sandwich, or spread bread with cream cheese or butter and place pear halves between the slices.

1980' and 1990's

PARMESAN PEARS WITH ROASTED CHICKEN

3 ripe pears
Salt
Oil or melted shortening.
3 chickens, halved
2 strips bacon
1/2 green pepper, diced
1/4 cup butter crumbs
1/4 cup grated parmesan

Rub chicken halves with salt, then brush with oil or melted shortening. Place in roasting pan, skin side down, on a broiling pan. Bake about 25 to 30 minutes at 350 degrees, then turn skin side up. Wash, halve and core pears. Place on broiler rack, cut side up with chicken and bake 25 minutes longer. Cook bacon until crisp. Remove from fat. Add green pepper and cook until tender. Break bacon into small pieces and mix with pepper, bread crumbs and cheese. Just before serving, spoon crumb mixture into cavities and cover cut surface of pear halves. Broil until mixture begins to brown. Serve with chicken. Makes 6 servings.

PICKLED PEARS

1 dozen pears, 4 cups water
2 cups sugar, 2 cups vinegar
1 stick cinnamon, ginger to taste
Whole cloves to taste

Peel pears, remove blossom ends but leave stems. Boil pears in 4 cups water until they can be easily pierced with straw. Remove pears and to juice add 3 cups sugar, 2 cups vinegar, 1 stick cinnamon, a little ginger and some whole cloves. Boil syrup 5 minutes, place in pears and continue boiling until syrup is thick. Carefully remove pears and pack in clean, hot jars. Boil syrup 5 minutes longer, remove spices, fill jars with boiling syrup and seal immediately.

PEAR BRUNCH FIZZ

1 large fresh Bartlett pear
1 cup finely crushed ice
1/2 cup heavy cream
2 egg whites
1/4 cup gin (2 ounces)
2 tablespoons superfine sugar
2 tablespoons fresh lime juice

Pare, core and dice pear to measure 1 1/2 cups. Turn into blender with all remaining ingredients. Whirl until well-blended. Makes 4 servings.

CLASSIC CONTEMPORARY RECIPES

PEAR AND SQUASH SAUCE

2 zucchini squash, cut into small cubes
1 red onion, diced
2 medium carrots, diced
1 jalapeno pepper, seeded, minced
3 tablespoons olive oil
3 ripe Bartlett pears, cored and diced
Tortilla Chips

Dice or cut zucchini, onion, carrots, pepper and pears. Add all together, add olive oil to moisten. Put into a blender and either pulse (for a chunkier result) or blend till smooth. Pour over freshly sliced pears or a fresh fruit salad. Whatever is on hand.

SLICED PEARS WITH PEAR VINAIGRETTE

2/3 cup fresh Bartlett pear
1/4 cup sugar
1/2 cup white wine vinegar or distilled white vinegar
1 teaspoon mustard
1/4 cup orange juice
3/4 cup vegetable oil
1/4 teaspoon salt
1/4 teaspoon black pepper

Combine the pear, sugar and vinegar in a small pan and cook over medium heat about 4 to 5 minutes. Remove from the heat and let cool. Puree the mixture in a blender, then add and blend in the mustard and orange juice. With the machine running, gradually drizzle in the oil. The dressing should become smooth and emulsified. Blend in the salt and pepper. Refrigerate until needed.

Serve over fresh sliced pears, or fresh fruit. Can also be used as a salad dressing or marinade.

SPAGHETTI WITH SAUTEED PEAR AND WALNUTS

1 large zucchini
1/2 tablespoon olive oil + more for drizzling
1/4 cup gorgonzola cheese + more for garnish
salt and pepper
1 small garlic clove, minced
1 Anjou pear
1/4 cup walnuts

Preheat the oven to 425 degrees. Prepare your pears by slicing them into eight pieces, making sure to remove all seeds. Lay the slices down on a baking tray and drizzle with olive oil and season with salt and pepper. Bake for 20-25 minutes, tossing the pears halfway through. Five minutes before the pears are done baking, throw the walnuts into the tray. When done, set aside.

Once you add the walnuts to the baking tray, place a large skillet over medium heat and add in the 1/2 tablespoon of olive oil. Once the oil heats, add in the garlic and cook for 1 minute. Add in the zucchini noodles, season with pepper and cook for about 1 minute or until they are heated through and start to soften.

Add in the gorgonzola cheese and cook for 1 minute, tossing to combine thoroughly. The cheese should fully melt into the noodles.

When the cheese is melted, place the noodles into a bowl. Top with pears, walnuts and extra gorgonzola.

STILTON AND WALNUT RAVIOLI WITH GRILLED PEARS

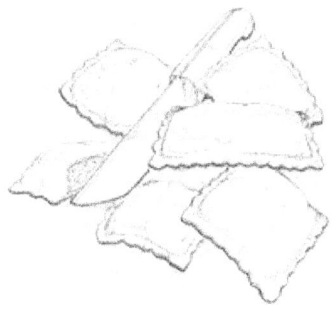

9 ounces fresh mini cheese ravioli
1/2 cup walnuts, toasted and chopped
5 tablespoons butter, divided
2 pears, peeled and diced
2 ounces' prosciutto
1/3 cup fresh sage leaves
1/2 cup Stilton

Cook ravioli according to package directions. Drain and set
aside. Melt one tablespoon of butter in skillet. Add diced pears and
cook until pears are soft, about 5 minutes. Remove pears from
skillet. Melt remaining 4 tablespoons of butter in skillet over medium
heat. When the butter just starts to turn brown, add the sage. Stir
constantly for approximately one minute. Immediately add the
ravioli, pears, prosciutto and walnuts. Stir to combine. Plate the pasta
and sprinkle with gorgonzola cheese.

CELERY AND PEAR BISQUE

4 1/2 tablespoons butter
6 cups thinly sliced celery with leaves (preferably organic; about 12 stalks) plus chopped leaves (for garnish)
18 ounces unpeeled ripe Bartlett pears, cored, diced (generous 3 cups) plus 1/2 cup finely diced (for garnish)
1 1/2 cups chopped dark green leek tops
3 small Turkish bay leaves
1 1/2 teaspoons chopped fresh thyme
1 1/2 tablespoons all-purpose flour
3 cups (or more) low-salt chicken broth

Melt butter in pot over medium-high heat. Add sliced celery, generous 3 cups diced pears, leek tops, bay leaves, and thyme. Cover; cook until celery softens, stirring occasionally, about 8 minutes. Toss in flour. Stir in 3 cups broth; bring to boil. Cover, reduce heat to medium-low, and simmer until celery is tender, about 20 minutes. Remove bay leaves from soup. Puree soup in batches in blender until smooth. Return puree to same pot. Season to taste with salt and pepper. Thin with more broth by 1/4 cupful's, if desired. Rewarm briefly. Divide soup among bowls; garnish with 1/2 cup finely diced pear and celery leaves.

PORK, PEAR AND WALNUT SALAD

1 tablespoon olive oil
1 pound pork tenderloin, cut into 1 inch cubes
1 tablespoon fresh chopped parsley
1 (10 ounce) bag fresh spinach leaves.
1 firm ripe Bartlett or bosc pear
1/4 cup chopped walnuts
1/2 cup balsamic vinaigrette salad dressing, or to taste.

Heat the oil in a large skillet over medium-high heat. Add the pork and parsley, cook and stir until pork is browned on the outside, and cooked through. Remove from the heat and set aside. Make a bed of spinach on individual serving plates or a large platter. Arrange slices of pear over the spinach. Top with cooked pork and sprinkle with walnuts. Drizzle the balsamic vinaigrette over the whole salad.

PEAR AND BLUE CHEESE TART

For the pastry:
2 cups all-purpose flour
1 teaspoon salt
5 tablespoons unsalted butter, cold
1 large egg

For the topping
2 large, firm pears, cut into thin wedges
3 ounces crumbled blue cheese, such as Stilton or Cambozola,
3 tablespoons olive oil
Sea salt
Crushed black peppercorns

For the pastry, combine the flour and salt in a large bowl. Cut it into the flour until there are just small pieces left. Quickly rub the butter into the flour with your fingers until combined. Add the egg and mix with the dough hooks of an electric mixer until crumbly. Form the dough into a thick disc, wrap it in plastic wrap, and freeze for 10 minutes. Preheat the oven to 400°F.

Take crust out of freezer and roll out into a disc, large enough to line the bottom and sides of a 12-inch quiche dish. Fit the dough, letting it hang over the rim a little or cut it off with a knife. Use a fork to prick the dough all over. Bake for 15 to 18 minutes or until golden. Arrange the pear wedges in overlapping circles on top of the warm, pre-baked pastry, sprinkle with the cheese, drizzle with the olive oil, and season to taste with sea salt and crushed peppercorns. Bake for 15 minutes or until the cheese has melted and the pastry is crisp. Enjoy warm or cold. Serves 8.

SLICED PEARS WITH PEAR VINAIGRETTE

2/3 cup fresh Bartlett pear

1/4 cup sugar

1/2 cup white wine vinegar or distilled white vinegar

1 teaspoon mustard

1/4 cup orange juice

3/4 cup vegetable oil

1/4 teaspoon salt

1/4 teaspoon black pepper

Combine the pear, sugar and vinegar in a small pan and cook over medium heat about 4 to 5 minutes. Remove from the heat and let cool. Puree the mixture, then blend in the mustard and orange juice. With the machine running, gradually drizzle in the oil. The dressing should become smooth and emulsified. Blend in the salt and pepper. Refrigerate until needed. Serve over fresh sliced pears, or fresh fruit. Can also be used as a salad dressing or marinade.

SPINACH, PEAR, AND FETA SALAD

2 firm ripe pears, cored and thinly sliced.
Place pears in bowl with 1 cup water, juice of small lemon, a couple of tablespoons to keep from turning brown. Set aside.
4 cups baby spinach,
1 shallot, finally chopped,
1/2 cup crumbled feta cheese,
1/2 cup slivered almonds,
1/2 cup raspberry vinaigrette dressing.

Place the baby spinach in serving bowl. Add shallot, feta and almonds. Drain pears and add to the salad. Toss gently to blend. Serve with raspberry vinaigrette dressing. Note May use any light vinaigrette dressing.

SCALLOPED PEARS

1/2 cup sugar
1/2 teaspoon cinnamon, ¼ teaspoon nutmeg
1 quart can of pears
1 lemon, juice and grated rind
2 cups bread crumbs
2 tablespoons butter

Add sugar and spices to pears and cook five minutes. Add grated rind and juice of lemon. Butter the crumbs. Arrange a layer of crumbs in a baking dish, spread with fruit mixture and continue until all ingredients are used. Have crumbs on top. Bake a half hour in a moderate oven until well browned. Serve with cream or any pudding sauce.

PEAR CRISP

2 cups fresh peaches or pears
1/3 cup soft butter
1 cup sugar
1 cup flour
1 teaspoon baking powder
1/2 teaspoon salt
1/2 cup milk
1 tablespoon cornstarch
1/4 teaspoon ground nutmeg
1 cup boiling water

Place pear slices (can be unpeeled) into 8x12 inch pan. Cream butter and ¾ cup sugar. Combine flour, baking powder, and salt. Add to creamed mixture alternately with milk. Spoon this mixture over the fruit. Sift 1 cup sugar, cornstarch, and nutmeg and sprinkle evenly over batter. Pour the hot water over top of mixture. Bake at 350⁰ for 60 minutes. The top will have a light crust appearance similar to a glazed donut. Best served with sweet whipped cream or vanilla ice cream.

FRESH PEAR CAKE

2 cups mashed fresh pears
1 cup shortening
1 1/2 cups sugar
2 eggs
2 cups flour
2 teaspoons cinnamon
2 teaspoons baking soda
1 teaspoon salt.

Topping:
½ cup brown sugar
1 cup chopped walnuts
I cup raisins (optional)

Cream shortening and sugar. Add eggs; beat until fluffy. Add dry ingredients; mix well. Add pear pulp and raisins; blend well. Pour into greased 9 x13 inch pan. Sprinkle topping over unbaked cake. Bake at 350 degrees for 30 to 40 minutes.

PEAR SCONES

1 ripe pear, peeled, cored and cut into pieces 1 1/2 teaspoon fresh
lemon juice
2 cups all-purpose flour
1 tablespoon sugar
1 tablespoon double acting baking powder
1/2 teaspoon baking soda
1/2 teaspoon salt
3/4 stick (6 tablespoons) cold unsalted butter cut into bits
3 to 6 tablespoons buttermilk
Egg wash made by beating 1 large egg with 1 teaspoon water

Puree the pear and lemon juice in food processor or blender until
smooth. Sift together flour, sugar, baking powder, baking soda and salt.
Add butter and blend until the mixture resembles coarse cornmeal. In a
small bowl beat the pear puree and 3 tablespoons of the buttermilk
until mixture is combined well. Add pear and buttermilk mixture to the
sifted flour mixture. Stir with a fork, adding more of the buttermilk if
necessary until it just forms a sticky but manageable dough. Knead the
dough lightly on a floured surface for 30 seconds and pat it gently into
a round 1 inch thick. Cut out rounds with a 2-inch cutter dipped in
flour and arrange the scones in a buttered baking sheet. Form the
scraps into a ball, pat the dough into a round 1-inch thick and cut out
scones in the same manner. Brush the tops of the scones with the egg
wash and bake in preheated 425 degree oven for 12 to 15 minutes until
lightly browned. Makes about 12 two inch scones.

PEAR CUSTARD PIE

1 unbaked 9-inch pie shell
5 cups ripe pears, peeled and sliced
1 cup sugar
1/4 cup butter
4 level tablespoons flour
2 eggs
1 teaspoon vanilla
Dash of ground nutmeg

Arrange pears in unbaked pie shell. Cream together sugar, butter and flour. Mix 2 eggs with vanilla. Add to cream mixture. Pour over pears. Bake at 350 degrees for 40to 50 minutes, till center is done. Stick a butter knife in center to test. Can prebake pie crust till just light brown, not all the way done. Fill and bake as directed. Do not overfill or it will take forever to get done.

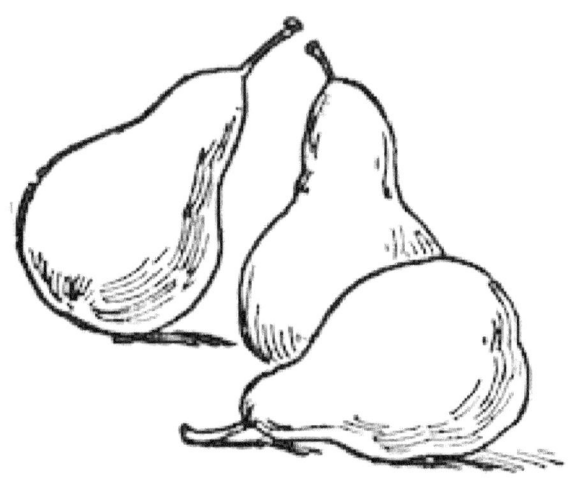

ABOUT THE AUTHORS AND EDITORS

Barbara Dahlberg, was born and raised in the Courtland area. Her father worked in the orchards and eventually for Greene and Hemley, now in their sixth generation of pear, apple and cherry farming. Her mother was a homemaker who fed Barbara's appetite for cooking and baking from scratch, allowing her to "swish the gravy" at ten and in charge of feeding the family by 12. Constantly on a budget, she learned that good stewards of the earth use everything they have, eventually becoming a master at preserving and gardening.

She met and married Jim Dahlberg, who soon became the lead salesman for Harvey Lymon Chemicals. The homemade cakes and breads she made for championship sporting events for her children caught the attention of the community. Soon she became the go-to person for wedding cakes.

In the early 1970s Jim and she were instrumental in getting a local pear festival off the ground, a multi-day event with a carnival, displays of pear equipment, food booths, and other activities to celebrate the pear harvest. By 1975 it evolved into the massive annual Pear Fair, attracting crowds, some years, of at least 30,000 people. While Jim began acquiring and preserving thousands of pear box labels from the region, Barbara decided to create **Pear Pearfection**, a cookbook featuring hundreds of recipes she collected from neighbors, the California Pear associations and growers and packers throughout the Delta.

When Jim fully retired, they moved to Amador County, where she took master gardening classes, and became president of the Amador County Master Gardeners. Recently, they moved nearer the Delta to Elk Grove, where they graciously continue to donate their time to the pear community. Jim donates twelve new pear labels from his massive collection for the Sacramento River Delta Historical Societies Annual Pear Label Calendar and Barbara has very generously allowed a revision and update of her now out of print and very rare book.

Maryellen Burns is director of A Cook's Tour of Sacramento, a Sacramento foodways project that chronicles the regions food and drink stories. A writer, editor, teacher, food sleuth and former caterer, she serves on the boards of the *Conference of California Historical Societies*, *Sacramento Book Collectors Club*, and *Sacramento River Delta Historical Society*. She is a member of *Les Dames d'Escoffier*, *Culinary Historians of Northern California*, *Slow Food* and other food, wine, and history associations. She is also author of *Lost Restaurants of Sacramento and Their Recipes* and two other food related books.

Tom Herzog has been a resident and third generation Delta farmer his whole life. His local family heritage dates to the late 1800's when his grandfather started farming at a ranch in the Pearson district of Courtland. Tom worked as shop manager and director for the family farm before he retired about six years ago, when the farm was sold. An avid used and rare book dealer and collector he now sales his wares at Locke's *Strange Cargo* store. A devoted volunteer, he's on the boards of the *Sacramento River Delta Historical Society*, current trustee (past 40 Yrs.) and President *Reclamation District 813*, the Pear Fair Committee and past director of the *Sacramento County Historical Society*, and founding member of *North Delta Conservancy*.

HOW TO PURCHASE ADDITIONAL COPIES

PEAR PEARFECTION is a collaborative project of the Sacramento River Delta Historical Society and the Courtland Pear Fair committee. Additional copies can be purchased from the Sacramento River Delta Historical Society. Bookstores, libraries and community groups can t E-mail: srdhs@riverdeltawireless.com, to purchase in quantity.

P.O.BOX 293
WALNUT GROVE, CA 95690
E-mail: srdhs@riverdeltawireless.com, website: www.srdhs.org

The Sacramento River Delta Historical Society is a non-profit organization created to preserve the historical heritage of the Sacramento River Delta, to promote a greater public awareness of Sacramento River Delta history, and to educate the public about the importance of the Sacramento River Delta's history.

The Resource Center is in the Jean Harvie Community Center in Walnut Grove and is open Tuesday mornings by appointment. It contains oral histories from the community, resource books, DVDS and transcripts from the general meetings, along with many collections donated by local Delta Residents.

The Pear Fair, is a non-profit organization and hosts a celebration of the annual Bartlett pear harvest in the picturesque, Sacramento River Delta region of California. Nestled along the Sacramento River, the town of Courtland is located 20 miles south of Sacramento on scenic Highway 160. Organized and run by a committee of local volunteers, it has become a long-standing summer tradition in the Delta that reflects the character and lifestyle of rural life, family fun, and is a wonderful day of entertainment, festivities, food and drink shared by all who attend each year. The Pear Fair Committee can be reached at PO Box 492, Courtland, CA 95615 email them at pearfaireats@gmail.com. Check out their website at: pearfair.com

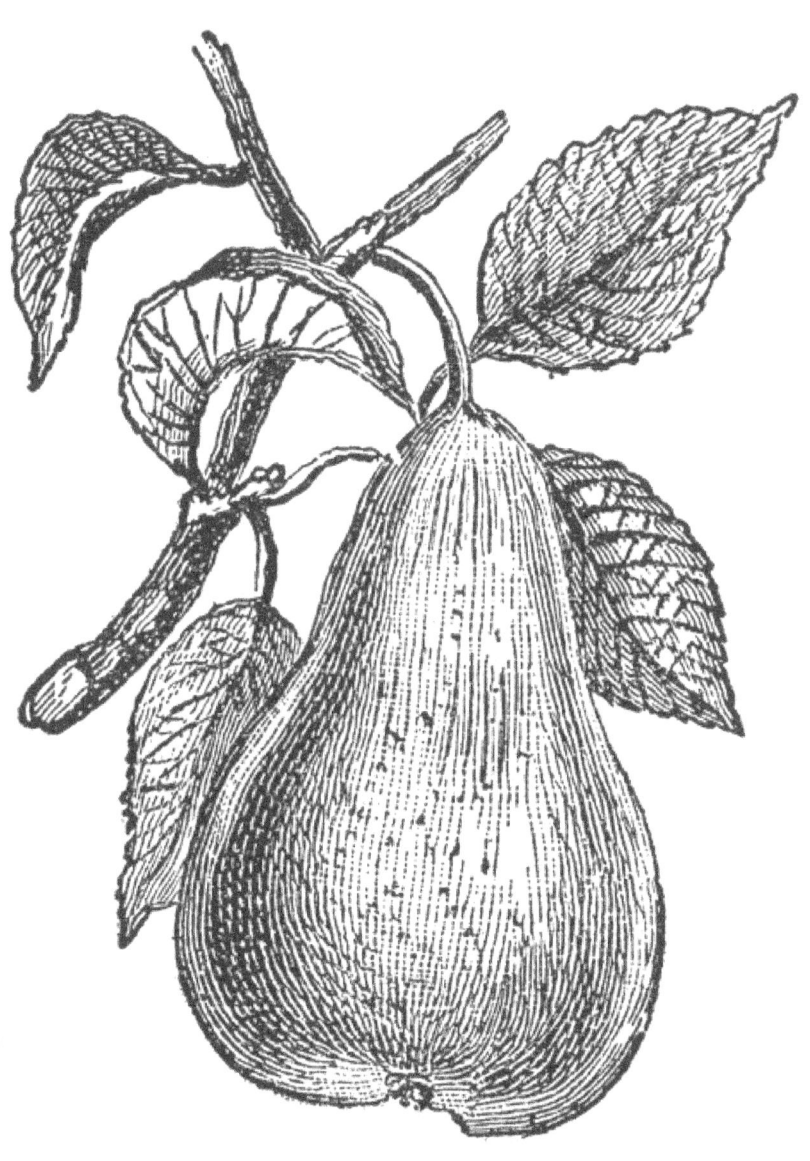

www.ingramcontent.com/pod-product-compliance
Lightning Source LLC
Chambersburg PA
CBHW071235130626
46556CB00003B/1018